"It is difficult to free fools from the chains they revere."
–Voltaire

Religion, including Christianity is a chain that billions of people revere. They reverence it because religious faith without fear seems impotent and all but impossible. Without necessarily knowing it, most Christians have more faith in their fears than they do in God, or they get the two confused.

Chandrika and I come from identical religious backgrounds and I relate to and resonate with the feeling and thoughts she expresses in this profoundly revealing journal of her journey to personal freedom and expanded consciousness.

The New and Now Heaven and the new and now earth are realized in redeemed (awakened) Consciousness. It is a reference to freedom from tradition, superstition and institutional religion.

The word apostate in both its Latin and Greek origin means: deserter or "runaway slave". The so-called "Apostate Church" will be made up of millions of people, like Chandrika who have fled organized religion's at least 2000 years of entrenched indoctrination and the psychosis, that has effected and infected the planet for millennia.

This book is a kind of underground railroad that has come above ground and is publicly helping people find freedom!
–Bishop Carlton Pearson

LORD, I DON'T WANT TO DIE A CHRISTIAN

LORD, I DON'T WANT TO DIE A CHRISTIAN

MY JOURNAL AND JOURNEY TO FREEDOM

CHANDRIKA D. PHEA

ONBRAND BOOKS

NASHVILLE, TENNESSEE

j.brand@wbrandpub.com
ONBrand Books
www.wbrandpub.com

Cover design by JuLee Brand / designchik.net

Lord, I Don't Want to Die a Christian /
Chandrika D. Phea —1st ed.

Available in Hardcover, Paperback, eBook and Kindle formats.

Hardcover ISBN: 978-1-950385-78-2
Paperback ISBN: 978-1-950385-61-4
eBook ISBN: 978-1-950385-62-1

Library of Congress Control Number: 2021941182

CONTENTS

MY JOURNEY

"GASP!" went my younger sister, after hearing the title of this book. "Well, what do you want to die as?!" she asked. To my surprise, her question made me realize we live in a world that, apparently, begs we die *as* or with religious identification.

But why not my sister's question? I was born one. Yes, I was born a Christian. All four of us, my sisters and I, were born Christians. Do I have to die one too? Must I die a Christian? These, and many more, are my questions.

My name is Chandrika Dianne Phea. As my birth certificate states, I was born a girl with brown eyes, six pounds, and six ounces. The certificate identifies me as Black because my parents have both been identified as such.

Why isn't religion included on a birth certificate? Shouldn't it be? Just as much as my parents were born or identified as Black, I am. My parents identify as Christians, so, quite naturally, their religious identity was my inheritance. Why not include religion on birth certificates?

The religion I know, the Black Church, is an entity all on its own. The Black Christian Pentecostal Church is another entity. We were raised *in* the Church of God in Christ. This denomination believes in the life, death, and resurrection of Jesus Christ. It embodies the charismatics of Blacks being endowed with the Holy Ghost. This denomination was born out of strife, if you will. The two excommunicated founders of the COGIC (Church of God in Christ) where unwelcomed because of their differences in belief from their Baptist association comrades. The denomination is listed with nearly five million members, twelve thousand congregations found in sixty other countries.

1

It is the fifth largest Christian church in the U.S., birthed out of disagreement and separation.

Eventually, as a college student, I secretly joined an Apostolic church. Sneaking was the only option, it seemed, because of the slight difference between the denomination I was raised in and the Apostolic Faith. Church of God in Christ baptize "In the name of the Father, Son, and Holy Spirit," according to Matthew 28:19. The Apostolic faith organization believes in baptizing in "Jesus' name," according to Acts 2:38. But my transitioning continued over to a non-denominational church, where I was licensed as a minister then ordained as a reverend.

My sisters and I grew up sitting on the first row of the church for a lot of our lives. Highland Drive Church of God in Christ was the first congregation I remember being a part of. This is where I was challenged to teach myself how to be a church drummer. My dad was the youth minister, so we were there plenty and, much of the time, the only youth present. Sunday school (Christian education), Sunday Night service (corporate worship), midweek service (Wednesday nights dedicated to studying the Bible), revivals (a series of Christian gatherings held to inspire active members of a church body to gain new converts), etc., were a part of our everyday lives. We grew up singing in the church, my sisters and I. We were the "Anointed and Appointed Phea Sisters," named after the national recording artists the "Anointed and Appointed Pace Sisters." My mother taught us the books of the Bible in a song, and we would recite them at church programs. Imagine four light-skinned, pigtail-wearing girls, standing on the steps of a pulpit, from oldest to youngest, reciting all sixty-six books of the Bible in sync. We were celebrities, so we thought. Today, I am still able to recite all sixty-six books.

As young ladies, we were active in the choir, youth activities, and filled vacant roles. I have been an usher, choir director, youth leader, and a few other things. My family was a part of a traditional church. For example, Communion Sunday (First Sunday), tithing, offerings, hymns, singing, shouting (dancing) were staples experienced as we gathered. There was really nothing more important to our existence. My sisters and I would get upset, shedding tears, if there was a Sunday we didn't go to church. Even in my late teens, being in church became such a personal priority, I'd leave my parent's home to attend gatherings intending to sneak back into the house because I was guaranteed to miss curfew.

Beyond school and family, church and church people are what we knew most. On the way to Sunday school one morning, I saw a neighbor outside cutting his yard. I couldn't believe it! It's Sunday! "Why is he outside cutting his yard?" I asked my mother. As a child, I was confused by the thought of our neighbor doing anything but going to church.

As was mentioned earlier, we were singers. I sang in the choir, on praise teams, in gospel groups, and in live gospel recordings. I have led worship workshops, been an armor bearer, and have preached on many occasions.

We come from a line of Pentecostal preachers. Both of our parents are pastors. I have three aunts and one uncle (a pastor) on my mother's side of the family who are preachers. Their parents were preachers.

I was to be like my grandmother, a national evangelist. Yeah, I heard that a lot growing up: "You are going to be just like your grandmother when you grow up!" It was something I loved hearing because I was crazy about the woman many referred to as "Mother Butler." She was Granny Butler to us. I will forever remember singing for her before she rose to preach, because as church culture would have it, a "sermonic solo"—to prepare the heart before the message—was the norm. And there I was, a little girl, sermonic soloing for my grandmother.

Sermonic solos were, back then, just one of many traditions I participated in. There was the sunshine band, junior church, baptism Sunday, tithing, offering, and I even preached my first sermon as a youth for Easter (another tradition). "Because He Lives, so Shall I" was the name of that sermon. I remember standing down on the floor in front of the pulpit under the podium because women could not stand where only men were allowed.

Speaking of women, as elementary students, we couldn't wear pants as boys do, another Pentecostal church tradition— no make-up or fingernail polish either. We walked to school often, in Oklahoma snow, wearing tights and leg warmers (hated those things). We continued that trek until my mother got fed up with the thought of her daughters walking in snow up to their knees—even if only for a few blocks. But it's what she and her sisters had done as children—wear skirts to school—just like their mother had done as a child.

I was destined to do what my grandmother did, even as I'd graduated from Beacon University with a Bachelor of Arts degree in Biblical Studies. I was ready to go from coast-to-coast with all I was raised to believe, with all I'd learned in college. But there came an interruption, an opportunity unlike any other I'd ever received.

I moved to China!

Me, a Pentecostal church kid, living and teaching in Henan, China? Unbelievable, to say the least. No one in my circle or immediate family had traveled internationally. What an amazing opportunity! This was a far cry from life as I'd experienced it in the States. Suddenly, my life changed from being an extremely devoted and active church member to getting off a bus in front of SIAS University.

While in-training for this job, I recall all of the preparation around culture shock, particularly for those of us who'd never been out of the country. The preparation was so much that I found myself praying culture shock wouldn't be my portion the first time I traveled abroad. Nevertheless, I moved into my assigned apartment on the second floor of the building designated for foreign staff, eager to experience this new life for a year in China. As we trained to teach incoming freshmen, I had already begun to sense a second-year commitment. It was very clear I was in the right place.

The first year of teaching, in a country where the freedom to gather at-will as Christians was and continues to be illegal, I initiated a weekly Bible study with two freshman college students that soon grew into a group of seven; David, Moony, Vivian, Tweety, Lean Bon, Felix, and Neil. This Bible study was held in my small, one-bedroom apartment so the group truly couldn't have grown much more. We chose to read through the book of Luke to introduce Jesus Christ and a relationship with him.

Reading each chapter of the book of Luke with students who were learning English was a two-year commitment and challenge. But, with the help of Chinese Bibles purchased for all these eager small group learners, we completed the book. It was a bit of a challenge, finding ways to provide understanding while keeping the culture of my Chinese students in mind. I can never forget reading through the New International Version of Luke chapter twelve to the fifty-first verse, "[51]Do you think I came to bring peace on Earth? No, I tell you, but division. [52]From now on there will be five in one family divided against each other, three against two and two against three. [53]They will be divided, father against son and son against father, mother against daughter and daughter against mother, mother-in-law against daughter-in-law and daughter-in-law against mother-in-law." Imagine explaining these verses to Chinese freshman college students whose culture thrives on the principles of family. It was tough.

During that journey, my students, who'd been so committed to showing up to the apartment weekly, reading the book of the Bible called Luke, knew nothing of my staying in China during my second Christmas and New Year holiday there. The first year, I traveled for the winter holiday, a western staff norm, because it would get so cold in Central China. Most of my comrades would travel south, where it was so much warmer. My first year in China, I traveled south to Hong Kong to continue in ministry and to stay warm. I lived in Hong Kong for two months at a twenty-four-hour prayer center, volunteering to keep prayer going twenty-four hours. When my two-month assignment ended, I traveled back to Central China to resume teaching and continue the study of Luke with my students. However, during year two, my second Christmas and New Year holiday vacation in Asia, I felt like God was calling me to stay put and spend that time with Him.

The need to stay in my freezing apartment, while many of my coworkers and friends traveled to warmer parts of the region, derived from my visit back to the States over the summer following the first-year commitment to SIAS. My visit to the church I was a member of before this foreign exposure was the craziest experience I'd ever had in a religious gathering.

It was my first weekend back in the States, the first Sunday of the month, Communion Sunday. As the congregation went through their normal routine, I experienced culture shock for the first time in my life! Yes, I'd gone to China, it being my first time leaving the country, but the predicted culture shock experience of leaving the States to live in another country wasn't my plight. The culture shock I experienced was that of going back to church. Returning to this deep-rooted practice, church, my life's culture, became overwhelming. I heard about the devil, saw the passing out of tithe and offering envelopes, and observed the preparation for Communion. For the first time in an entire year, I realized I'd lived without hearing, "The enemy in your life (devil)," without tithing, and without participating in Communion. It scared me. I thought, *Oh my God! I am going to hell!* But the truth was, for the entire first year of living in China, I'd experienced the blessing of God like I never had before. It was mind-blowing to fathom how I was being crazy blessed while, as an international educator, my participation in the religious practices were extremely limited. I had so many questions. I lived in a building occupied by western and international Christians so why hadn't I heard about the devil? Many of us had been participators in Communion, yet no one knocked on my door and said, "It is First Sunday; let us prepare for Communion." No one policed what I did with my small teacher's salary, making sure that I *gave ten percent to God.*

"If I wasn't doing any of this, what *had* I been doing?" was the question I asked God.

A word of advice: Don't ask God a question in sincerity and expect not to get an answer in return. God's answers are what inspired me to read the Bible in its entirety. By this time, I had already graduated from college with a Bachelor of Arts Degree in Biblical Studies and was a licensed minister. Bible commentaries, Bible dictionaries, and more lined my bookshelves. But I felt challenged to read as my students were reading. These freshman college kids didn't have access to and couldn't afford the extra biblical resource materials. Page by page, book by book, I read. I cried, got angry and confused many days, but I wouldn't, or more truthfully, *couldn't* stop until I finished.

There was so much I was doing, so much I was being, and so much I believed that wasn't in this Bible I was reading. So much of what I practiced, for the sake of the Christian faith, wasn't in this book Christians use as its authoritative guide. As someone who had a concentrated education and an ordination certificate, I had less clarity than I'd ever had before. I found myself questioning the authors of these books, only to realize I should have been asking questions all along.

While reading and believing in God, I learned that having a relationship with God doesn't mean to stop thinking for myself. God doesn't expect me to lose my imagination or trade my intellect in for faith. The absence of certainty I had after reading the last sentence, "Amen," left me with one question.

God, now what do I do?

God: "Can you just love me and love people?"

Yes!

Finding inconsistencies and holes in many of the Biblical stories I'd come to own left me with a significant lack of clarity. But to love God and people was without question and seemed easy enough—so I thought. As this new journey began, I learned that loving people would be a challenge. I loved God already, as much as possible, but I had no clue about this "loving people" thing.

I started by revisiting subjects of society that isolated me from people who believed differently from fundamental Christian teachings. I had to stop seeing others as *them*. I had to learn "their" differences and respect them rather than putting effort into making people be like me. This "re-education" would make it easier to love my neighbor.

This new direction awakened me to one major reality: Christianity was keeping me from doing what God really wanted of me; to love others. Christianity was a hindrance to me doing exactly what Jesus taught.

I found myself torn between choosing the greatest of all the laws and remaining a Christian. It felt like loving God *and* people while being a Christian was impossible. Choosing this new commandment given by Jesus meant losing lots of religion-initiated relationships with people I loved, losing the spotlight as a part of my organized religion experience, losing the significance found in roles assigned to me in the construct of church services, losing recognition for being talented, etc. However, this experience of freedom and love looked much greater. I was ready to decide.

What you read in this journal is the process of stripping away Christianity as I learned and came to know it. You will read of my journey to freedom and love for God, making it impossible to continue in Christianity. I have walked through this unraveling of religion while maintaining a relationship with God. I believe this ongoing process will last my entire life and it is one that I desire to share with people of all religions and faiths.

The following is a peek into my journey from the fig leaves of Christianity. Each discovery, revelation, and question shared represents the removal of a fig leaf from my life. And by fig leaf, I mean cover. At the end of each journal entry, a part of who God created me to be is revealed. You will see my evolution as I revisit original journal entries and offer a new perspective in a dated postscript.

The womb is limited in space and expansion, so just as we all outgrew it, I've grown out of the religion I was born into. The same appreciation I have for the womb of my mother, is also owed to Christianity. If it were not for the Christian faith, I wouldn't have my relationship with God. But, just as the womb is after nine months of embryo growth to birth, Christianity is now too small for the reflection and expression of God I've been called to.

I desire your participation in the revealing of freedom, so there are journal pages available for you to add your thoughts and questions.

Your curiosity has company.

Join me in the journey.

MY CHINESE NAME

My 10 a.m. Oral English class asked if I had a Chinese name. I thought this would be the perfect homework assignment: choose a Chinese name for me. My students were to select a name individually, include the meaning, and I would choose the one I found most fitting. The next class period, when homework was due, only a few actually did the assignment. I gave an extension, of course, but was displeased by the lack of attention given to the project. Having done the homework on time, one of my students approached me during the break and said, "I did my homework, and I want you to see it." She showed me the Chinese name—*Chang Fei.*

The name means *Freedom!* This was the first name presented. To be fair to the other students, I wanted to wait for them to turn in their name choices before announcing my decision. But *Chang Fei* was sold to the woman who was determined to walk in complete freedom, the freedom intended for me, in this life. God is bigger than us.

P.S. JANUARY 19, 2018
At the moment of this experience, I had no idea of the freedom ordained for me, but I did know that going to China was freedom from what I'd known, from the disappointment and heartbreak I'd experienced in Columbus, Georgia. Even as I type this, I realize there is a freedom *from*, and a freedom *comes!* A freedom *from* is, as I define it, a freedom worked for. Freedom *comes*, in my mind, is an inherent freedom—a freedom that comes with our arrival into the world. If this is

true, when or at what point was this inheritance lost? Freedom *comes* is that space in time between our first cry as a newborn baby and when we respond to our given name. That name given to us, often agreed upon by two different people with two different life experiences, two different perspectives of life, is the beginning of being "swaddled." Just as a blanket given at birth, we are swaddled by their expectations of us, their morals, living up to the meaning of the name given, and their religious beliefs, if any. On July 6, 2015, I made note of a question that read, "Knowing now what you know of yourself, what name would you give yourself?" I absolutely love my given name, the uniqueness of it. Still, I look back, being aware of that space in time between my first cry as an infant and the first time I responded to my given name called, imagining what name, expectations, and standards would I have assigned to my individuality, as I now know it.

Are you curious?

Date: _____

...TO BE A GIRL!

DECEMBER 19, 2007

I encouraged one of my Bible reading participants to read Proverbs after finding her boyfriend had another girlfriend (*whatever*). My response to this unfortunate event was, "Good! These actions were in his heart from the beginning. You don't want anyone with that kind of mess in his heart. What is in his heart at the start is what comes out later. So good, I am glad you found out now." I expressed to her the importance of knowing how valuable she is, and then, to seal the deal, I asked her to read, specifically, Proverbs 31. At class tonight, I asked for an update on what she read. And I quote, "The Bible is right." I asked her what she was thinking while she read it. "I thought, I felt very good to be a girl," she said.

You guys, I really don't know what to do with myself right now! Exciting!

P.S. DECEMBER 29, 2017

If only I could offer an apology for this pure but religious response to what was, most likely, a broken heart. Not long before landing at Beijing International Airport, for one of the most significant changes of my life, I'd called off the engagement to the first man I'd ever been in love with. My heart hurt in my chest for over a year.

I was so busy being a Christian I'd forgotten that part of my story, as this young student confided in me about her pain. Surely God didn't expect me to replace this painful segment of my personal narrative with stories read of in the Bible.

Could religion be a thief of the human story?

Are you curious?

Date: _____

WHAT ABOUT PETER?!

DECEMBER 19, 2007

One of my students asked me to name his newborn nephew. I asked him to get a picture of the baby to me, and I would do my best to do as requested. In the meantime, I talked to God about it. I received the picture and at first sight of the boy, I thought, *Peter*! I emailed my student the name as such, "Peter . . . He walked on water!" He told his sister, and she was very pleased. While on break, he added Simon to Peter. I changed the spelling to Symon and my student loved it! I was able to share with him why I chose Peter, the man who walked on water. That's good quality time with a student, if ya' know what I mean. He called his sister, who lives in another big city in China, and shared the story with her. I spoke to her, told her how to spell it, she wrote it down, and was very grateful! I wish you guys could have seen my student's face as he shared the story with his sister. He laughed with so much joy . . . she did too.

This is exciting to me because most of my students came to college without an English name. This boy will grow up knowing his English name, knowing who he is, and he will share the story behind it.

P.S. JANUARY 2, 2018

Now, when hearing, "I wanted my baby to have a Bible name" today, I am even more intrigued. Those of whose books we read of in the Bible didn't have "Bible names." How much more empowered would my student have felt, had I taken this opportunity to encourage him to find an English name for his nephew? Would my student have been prouder by looking at the same picture and perceiving an English name that would fit their new family member's character? My heart was pure, but I was too busy being a Christian.

Are you curious?

Date: _____

HIS REFLECTION

Yesterday, I was having a conversation with one of my Hong Kong friends. "What is it with these cursing Christians?" I asked. She said she does not mind cursing, that it's *legalism* that Christians don't curse. I shared my opinion and moved on. I prepared to settle myself for bed and prayer last night, and it came up again. "Why do you think it's not okay to curse as a Christian?" The sentiment "I was raised to believe it is wrong," doesn't work anymore for this current generation of young people.

God reminds me of this: Let's just say I had my own Adam moment. I want God to look at me and find Himself, to find His reflection in me. I want Him to find me and say, "In her I am well pleased." Here is the problem. I don't know when He will come looking. It wasn't scheduled when God came down in the cool of the day looking for Adam. He just showed up. When He was calling Adam, He wasn't looking for Adam, He was looking for Himself! The only thing scheduled the day that Jesus was baptized, that they knew of, was just that, baptism. God opening heaven to find His son and send His sign of approval was not foreknown.

Secondly, if God can find His reflection in me, the world can. People must see Jesus in me so being cautious about where I am, who I am with, what I am doing and saying is very critical. I don't know when God will send people looking for Jesus. The Lord has got to be able to see me as a reflector of His image.

Well, back to the drawing board. I've got self-work to do.

P.S. JANUARY 19, 2018

This entry is funny to me now because nothing gets me to cursing like the subject of religion. I don't believe God is moved by cursing. However, my preference is not to use such language because it is a poor representation of what my mother taught her children—what it means to be a lady. God is not offended if I curse but my desire is to mirror my mother's femininity. In this regard, how I reflect her matters more.

Are you curious?

Date: _____

THE EVIDENCE OF INTIMACY

FEBRUARY 24, 2008

"WOW! You guys are an awesome couple! How did you meet?"

Well, I had been seeing Him around, ya' know, in different places. I would see Him doing what He does, but I never really got involved. I'd stand off to the side, unnoticed, so I thought. It would be enough to just watch Him interact with other people. But I wouldn't see Him often; seeing Him was reliant on sincere invitations of His presence to the places I visited often. As a matter of fact, when I knew I was going where He would be, I'd try to prepare myself, although, as I said before, I would just stand off to the side and watch Him.

One day I had an appointment, that night actually: it was a rehearsal. It was a rehearsal for a CD release concert. Evening came, I arrived sort of late, so I sat back a couple of rows from the singers. I was a bit distracted because of where I had just come from, and I hate being late. I didn't even notice Him there right away. Eventually, the rehearsal was over. I remember the last song the group sang, "My Worship for My Love."

Most everyone left, all but two people. I was sitting there in a section of the building alone, and from nowhere, He approached me. As I've already mentioned, I didn't even notice Him there immediately, so it was a big surprise. It completely caught me off guard! Instantly I could feel His love for me! There was no resisting Him! *It was love at first sight*! He wrapped His arms around me, hugging me gently at first. It was as if He wanted to do more but had to hold back because He knew the power of His strength. I appreciated His thoughtfulness. Naturally, I embraced Him in return. Really, I just couldn't resist. But when

I reached into His arms and let all of my inhibitions go, He squeezed me, bringing me even closer to Him! I couldn't take it!

I let go very gently, got myself together, put my coat on and got my belongings, as if to say, "Well, it was nice meeting you." I stood to pick up my things still feeling the embrace of His arms. I walked away with tears in my eyes. His gentleness was felt for only a second but then He squeezed me so hard that I could not stand! I fell to the floor because the rhythm of each step taken did not match His height and width. Finally, I gave up! I just let Him love me. I couldn't fight Him anymore. He was too strong, entirely too big, and too hard to resist. Eventually, I said to Him, "Would you please let me go?"

When He did let me go, I had to be helped up, my things had to be carried, along with me, to my car! It has been from that night until now that I have been in love with Him. I now realize that when noticing Him, thinking I was going unnoticed, He noticed me before I even knew of His existence in this manner.

I was sitting out at the ocean the other day looking at what He had done, and just looking at it, made me blush. After more than eight years, He is making me blush. There's a first time for everything I guess . . . gosh, I love Him. God and I are in the stage of our relationship that I'd call, The Evidence of Intimacy.

P.S. JANUARY 17, 2018

This experience, and others of the same kind, made me unafraid to explore and ask God questions of the many narratives told by Christianity. And I *still* blush at the sight of the reflection of God's glory.

Are you curious?

Date: _____

DREAM PREPARATION

FEBRUARY 28, 2008

My students and I have just finished our first week of the second semester. It's been kind of a normal week, but I wanted to share this with you.

After being in Hong Kong for a month, I returned to challenge my students even more to prepare for their dreams. Let me explain. Most of my students said, "ooh" and "ah," when they heard I had the opportunity to go to Hong Kong. They said, "It is my dream to go to Hong Kong." But while in Hong Kong, I realized most of my students are not prepared for their dream.

Mainland China, as some of you may know, is not the cleanest place. Littering is said to be a part of the culture. I'm not talking a little trash here and there; I'm talking about being on the bus and the young lady across the aisle finishes her banana and throws the peel in the aisle. It is nothing to walk on the main street and step over whatever you want to imagine. I was walking down the street the other day and saw a father lift his sons up on top of a brick wall; the boys opened their zippers and urinated over top of it, all on the main street. Parents will stop what they are doing, shopping perhaps, take their children outside to the sidewalk and let them urinate on the sidewalk, and as I hear, they will even have bowel movements in the park. When I go in my classrooms, normally the desks are overwhelmingly full of trash, food, used Kleenex, fruit peelings, etc.

The other thing most of my students do, placing blame on the culture, is spit everywhere. It's nothing to walk up the stairs to class, trying to avoid the spit of someone who just hacked it out of their throat as they walk in front of you. I am writing on the chalkboard in the heat of my lesson when suddenly, I hear the preparation of someone ready to spit on the floor of my class-room. I have even been in a restaurant sitting next to a student who hacked and spit it out right there at the table. And please be clear, my students and others feel this is the culture. But I go to Hong Kong, where the population is more than ninety percent Chinese, and find out if someone spits there, as my students do, it is a $5,000 Hong Kong Dollar fine. Even so for littering, $5,000 HKD!

I spent time painting a picture in your mind so you can under-stand, as clearly as possible, this entry. My mother taught me, in essence, bad habits don't change because you are in a new place. "If you will do it here, you will do it there," she'd say. I came back to my students and asked this question of each of them, "Do you dream of going to Hong Kong? Yes or no, and why?"

I have eight classes with no less than twenty-five students in each class. I would say ninety-five percent of my students said yes, they did want to go to Hong Kong. The largest response given was, "*It's clean with clear skies!*" If a student wanted to go anywhere else in the world it would have been for the same rea-son, including green grass and clear water. These young people had no clue I was setting them up to introduce to them the lit-tering fine of $5,000 HKD.

Written on the board were some of the reasons for want-ing to visit their dream destination. Then I wrote on the board, "$5,000 HKD," asking the students to tell me what they thought the amount meant. Some of them said it takes that amount of money to travel there, some mentioned shopping, some guessed it as the cost of living. Needless to say, when I finally told them about the fines, they were astonished. I further explained to them that if I had said, "We are all going to Hong Kong tomor-row," I would need to take thousands of dollars to cover the fines received because of the lack of readiness. It is said that the citizens of Hong Kong don't like it when mainland China citizens visit because of their choices to follow through with the bad habits. *Not my students!* I pointed out some reasons I thought littering and spitting in undesignated areas is not just cultural but a choice: "My mother and father did it, so I do it . . . everyone else does it so . . ." I further explained my desire to help this future generation dream bigger than ever. Much of the previous semester was spent building their self-esteem, confidence, and coaching them to dream bigger because, "If you dream big, you will do big" (my famous quote). These students practice said quote with me, but now that they are dreaming bigger, it's time to prepare them for the day their dreams come true. I challenged them all not to spit on the floor, the ground, and not litter, for one week, in the buildings, classrooms, in their bedrooms, around women, and on the sidewalks. We talked about the pollution problem in China and how it has become a concern for those participating in the Olympics. My students can't fix the greatest part of the problem but as I shared with them, "You can help where you are. If you change, you will teach your children differently and they will teach *their* children differently."

After receiving the challenge to change, one of my students stopped me while walking to Peter Hall and said, "I promise I will throw all trash in the rubbish, and I will go and teach my father this. You are right, it's a choice. This makes me think about other things of the culture that is really a choice."

My job was done.

P.S. JANUARY 16, 2018

By sharing this experience of my attempt to shift a cultural mindset and in publishing this memoir, I make the same effort. Documenting and publishing my journal and journey to freedom is not an endeavor to change the cultural mindset of Christianity but the cultural mindset of the world as it relates to religion. This journal entry may help those who will, when hearing the title of this book, conclude that Christianity hurt me.

It didn't hurt me.

Christianity hindered me.

To be continued . . .

Are you curious?

Date: _____

A WHOLE MOOD

MARCH 1, 2008

Every Sunday, we have a youth outreach at 10:30 a.m. There is music, testimonies, and sharing from the heart of our Father. In most cases men do the singing, facilitating, most of the testimonies, and yes, of course, the sharing of God's heart. This is not a surprise to me but seeing that I was hired because of whose I am, my educational background, and experience in the work of the Father, the whole *man* issue is a bit magnified to me. My concern isn't about me or what I can and cannot offer to this time, which is called Power Hour. What concerns me is how, for my students, especially the ones I have been assigned to empower, will view this hierarchy. My students are impressionable young college men and women. Keeping female students in mind, we, as instructors, are strongly encouraged by this same outreach organizer to be available to our students after these events, as they ask questions needing, perhaps, further instruction. The students are given what is called a "walking question." The speaker or facilitator gives the students questions to ask their professor as they walk back to the campus after Power Hour.

The issue is that myself and others, consistently provide instruction as it pertains to the heart of God, then take our students, women included, to this event and all they see are men standing before them. It's been on my heart to approach the organizer about my concern, so I finally did tonight.

How about this one! 1) No one has ever asked "Why only male speakers?" As a matter of fact, no one has even asked the predecessor. 2) He's Lutheran and this I knew before approaching him. 3) His response was, "I never noticed the inconsistencies." I pointed out the fact that we as women are qualified enough to come here and teach, highlighting that most of us were chosen because of our heart for God (not our teaching abilities or the lack thereof).

I and others like me consistently provide guidance and leadership with the heart and leading of our Father's word, but we would bring our students to outreach where they see only men. In all fairness, sometimes we see women doing some "house cleaning while the men go to work," that is, preparing and passing out music, facilitating (I've seen once or twice) when the men are not available to do so, but as the organizer admitted, for the most part, it is all men.

"I don't believe this is a good example in a society where men and women are seen as equals," I said. I also offered a reminder that there are more women in the roles of pastoring here in China than there are men.

He said he is going to pray about it and invited me to a student meeting where I would be asked to share my sentiments.

The privilege of instructing a group of students has been given to me by God. In that group, plus a few who are considering joining, are students with major leadership characteristics. I spend time with these leaders, consistently mentoring them. Three or four of these students are girls with very evident leadership qualities, so my heart is to empower them mentally, emotionally, and spiritually. I want them to know they can *do* and *be* anything they desire, which includes doing the work of the Lord.

Pray for me, I am in the challenging mood.

P.S. JANUARY 18, 2018

I know, I know, I know. Paul, the apostle, wrote a letter to the church of Corinth in which he included instruction about women in the church, admonishing them to be quiet, referencing the law.

If it were Apostle Paul partnering in ministry with me in China, if Paul organized Power Hour, if he headed the board of men overseeing this gathering, I would have presented the same concerns and inconsistencies to him . . . in a letter.

Are you curious?

Date: _____

ORDINATION SPEECH

MARCH 4, 2008

I was asked to share some of my life accomplishments.

My first accomplishment is coming to the realization that there is no love greater than the love of God. After God seemingly came out of Heaven to rescue me from religion, bringing me into a relationship with Him, I made the irresistible commitment to spend the rest of my life getting to know Him. What an accomplishment! The second significant accomplishment in my life is that of obedience to God despite my struggles, despite the opinions of others, and despite lack, from which God has delivered me. I have not always immediately submitted to God, but I have learned and continue to learn that God's Word is true, "Obedience is better than sacrifice." It is for this reason, along with the grace and favor of God, that He woke me up at 4:30 in the morning and said of me, "Ordained."

So, lastly but always first in my life, thank You God, for your seal and signature of approval.

There you have it, my life accomplishments.

—Chandrika

P.S. JANUARY 4, 2018

It is crazy, the reminder of becoming an ordained Christian minister, and it must be mind-blowing to read this journal entry while anticipating the next. I imagine reality completely apart from what I've been taught about religion. It seems as though Christianity strips one of its curiosities about God, the world, and how all this works. It is written that Jesus encouraged us to become like little children. My sense of curiosity is coming more alive as I continue to shed Christianity.

Are you curious?

Date: _____

IF I HAD BEEN ASKED

MARCH 25, 2008

"What is worship to you?"

Worship embodies the true freedom of my soul; it is where my soul lives. Worship is literally what houses my spirit. This house has no walls. It has no ceiling, no floors, not even doors. These things would be bondage for true freedom. Yes, I did say this house has no walls, ceilings, floors, and no doors, yet I am free to move about in any form I see fit. I can move about naked, baring all. For the days I am more aware of what I am carrying or what I am wearing, even in this place of full exposure, it's okay, I won't be evicted, this house has been paid for.

There are no clocks in this house, so there is no time kept. No time kept, means no agenda. No agenda means no schedule. The address of this place of dwelling is In the Beginning Freedom Lane. When God created me, He designed this place, and I wouldn't trade this space.

Home is where my bed is and this is my soul's truth; where worship is, my soul lives. Worship is where the core of my being is at rest. It is my reason for living, worship. I do not have children or a spouse to wake up to—my only care is for this house my soul lives in. It does require maintenance, this house, so the Word of God helps me maintain this place of truth. In recent days, I've not given many invites to my house. Life has caused me to put a "Do Not Disturb" sign on the door that does not exist. However, when God, the one whom I worship, is ready, He will remove the sign and there won't be anything I or anyone else can do to stop Him. I have also stated lately, "If I don't have my relationship with God, I cannot live," worship.

To answer a question not asked of me, "What is worship to you?"

Worship is home, and there's no place like it.

P.S. FEBRUARY 7, 2018

This question was asked of the music ministry team I was once a part of. In response to the inquiry, I was intrigued enough to sit down at the place of imagination and articulate what I saw. I have heard that the ultimate expression of worship is obedience to a God-given command, submission, and giving. I have also heard that the ultimate expression to God is *serving*. But personal evolution leads me to believe that the ultimate expression of worship to God is *being*—being whom He created me to be. It is doing what He created me to do, *being* my purpose, and therefore *doing* my purpose. If I were asked, today, "What is worship to you?" Worship is doing what I've been created to do, what I am purposed to do and that is, to just be.

Are you curious?

Date: _____

GOD KEEPS DOING IT!

MAY 18, 2008

Two of the boys in my small group accepted Jesus today! You have no clue how pumped I am right now.

Keep us in your prayers.

P.S. FEBRUARY 25, 2018

It is so interesting to read this now because I have absolutely no interest in winning souls. I know, it is written in Proverbs "he that wins souls is wise." But the writer says it's *wise* not a *must.* To add, I just don't know what it means: what is it to "win a soul?"

Furthermore, why didn't Jesus go about leading people to accept him into their hearts? Why didn't Jesus go around inviting people into relationship with him? While typing out these questions, I can hear the echo of, "Jesus hadn't died yet. He hadn't shed his blood yet. His shed blood was needed for the remission of sins." Then I am led to a couple of other questions: What happened to all of those gone in death before Jesus? What was their existence after death?

But, beyond all of the questions above, why does the soul need to be "won"? How has the soul been lost? How has the soul, which is intangible or immaterial, been manipulated? Why is the soul broken? How did what cannot be touched become fractured?

I just wonder if we've behaved accordingly because we have bought into the idea of coming into this world broken. Imagine being taught differently. Imagine believing when we came to the world, the soul, created by God, is complete and cannot otherwise be. Can the soul and its construct, be interrupted by one who did not create it? Can anything we do or don't do mold or break us—mold or break the soul?

We read of the psalmist David, "I was born in sin and shaped in iniquity." The interesting thing about his sentiment is I've heard it preached, not quoted, many times over, "*We* were born in sin and shaped in iniquity." But it is written of David to have said of himself, "he" was born in sin and shaped in iniquity. Who told him he was born in sin? Who said he was shaped in iniquity? That is something he had to have been taught, right? Isn't it like being told you were born Black, White, Hispanic, Jewish, or the like? We don't come out of our mother's belly knowing we were born to a race or religion. Rather, these things were learned.

As an ordained reverend in the Christian church, having earned a degree from a biblical university, I am over "winning souls to Christ." As is written, Jesus commanded his disciples to preach the good news and good news is all I've got.

Are you curious?

Date: _____

BUT THEY ARE SUPPOSED TO BE!

DECEMBER 13, 2008

I have heard this quote and even said it time and time again: "His ways are not our ways, and His thoughts are not our thoughts, His ways are higher than ours." In fact, I have heard it twice this week, and God followed up with an intriguing response.

Isaiah writes, "Seek ye the Lord while he may be found, call ye upon him while he is near: Let the wicked forsake *his way, and the unrighteous man his thoughts: and let him return unto the Lord,* and He will have mercy upon him; and to our God, for He will abundantly pardon. *For My thoughts are not your thoughts, neither are your ways My ways, said the Lord.* For as *the heavens are higher* than the earth, *so are My ways higher* than your ways, *and My thoughts than your thoughts.*"[1]

It is when the world's chaos isn't understood, that I've heard this scripture preached from pulpits but I don't believe the text was meant to be a reference point to provide comfort in times of devastation. The height of the Father's ways and the height of His thoughts are compared to how high heaven is above the Earth. When hearing someone say, "His ways are not our ways and His thoughts are not our thoughts, His ways are higher than ours," I heard God in response, "**BUT THEY ARE SUPPOSED TO BE!**" His thoughts are supposed to be our thoughts and His ways are supposed to be our ways. How else are we going to reflect Him on the Earth?

My prayer is that through His spirit, alive in me, I am found trading my thoughts for His thoughts and trading my ways for His ways that I might be made into the image of His son, to which this is my ultimate purpose.

---

1 I have chosen to emphasize in italics the words and phrases from this passage which I find to be exceptionally important.

Are you curious?

Date: _____

SPIRIT OF REJECTION VS. FEAR OF REJECTION

JANUARY 29, 2009

I have finally come to accept rejection as a normal part of life rather than praying against the *spirit* of rejection, often taught over many religious platforms. Because we have freedom to choose, we will reject, and we will be rejected. Embracing the aforementioned has been an introduction to another level of personal freedom.

The *fear* of rejection makes more sense to me. Praying, accepting this, renders more peace versus praying for God's deliverance from being possessed by the spirit of rejection, which just doesn't seem like a real thing. I've not been *given* the *spirit* of fear, but a spirit of love, power, and a sound mind. Fear is something picked up as a result of sin, so the fear of rejection is worth the work to conquer.

P.S. APRIL 27, 2017

The feeling we call rejection is, as I see it, actually that of reaping the harvest of someone else's "no."

I believe every decision we make is a seed sown. If every decision made is a seed sown, every decision made yields fruit; a decision made yields results. When others have offered a "no" in a variety of ways, those "nos" are decisions made. If refusal is a decision made, that decision "not to" is a seed sown and yields fruit. The question we should now ask is, "Whose return is it? Whose seed has yielded fruit?" The results of one's decisions belong to the one making the decision. The "no" of said decision maker is their seed in the ground. Isn't it the decision maker who reaps the results of its "no" or "not to"? If so, to internalize rejection as one on the other side of a "no," would be to harvest (gather, reap) the fruit or results of the decision. Wearing rejection as a result of someone's decision "not to" is equivalent to going to someone else's field, watching them plant seeds, waiting to reap the results of what they've sown.

For years, I wore the notion of spirit of rejection as was taught by influential Christian clergy. But I realized, rejection isn't a spirit or something my spirit suffered from. It was my perspective of someone else's choice that my spirit was "suffering" from.

We do not have to reap of the "no" from another. From this point on, I'll be careful of internalizing rejection as a result of another's freedom to choose "not to." The freedom to choose has nothing to do with my personal desire. There won't be a need to buy books about how to get over what holds little to no sustenance, the spirit of rejection, or a need to stand in another prayer line with an eagerness to be free.

It is too simple.

Give others the room to choose and allow them to harvest the fruit of their "not to."

Are you curious?

Date: _____

WHAT IF?

MARCH 12, 2009

I know the experience of working the drive-thru. You stand there listening to voice after voice telling you what is wanted or needed. "Hello, what can I get for you today?" "Hi, how can I help you?" Then there is a voice, alone, that responds with the reason for being there. "Yes, I would like . . ." or "I need . . ."

What if Jesus worked the drive-thru? This place in my imagination comes from the fact that my brother Christian, who was found dead about three weeks ago, worked a Burger King drive-thru in Columbus, Georgia. I imagine that when the voice on the other side of that drive-thru asked what they needed or wanted Christian did not take into consideration of what lay behind the voice: race, current wrong-doings, past mistakes of the person behind the voice, the gender, age, etc. If the person had money to pay for what was asked for, for what was wanted or needed, Christian, like so many others who have the same occupation, served each person with excellence. I wonder if Christian had known the past, present, and future mistakes, failures, imperfections, offenses, and faults of those he was assigned to serve, would he refuse to serve them and put them off on some other business? "You have way too many needs, too many issues, go next door, call the next person . . ." Even if they had the money would he not have served them because of who he knew them to be?

Imagine the scene with me, standing there in the drive-thru listening to the voices of people with needs. You are there hearing the needs of the person, ready to offer your services. You don't know what the person looks like, what their family background may be, religious choice or the lack thereof, race, past mistakes, current pressures, future outlooks, offenses, or the pain they may have caused their loved ones. You just stand there ready to offer your services to a person who says, "I need" on the other side of the drive-thru. Let's take a break from the drive-thru and walk over to the front counter. Come on, use your imagination. What do you see? More than voices, huh? Yeah, I know. Here's a question for you: Now that you know a little more, will it affect how you serve the person on the other side of the counter? Now that there is a face, race, gender, class, moral perspective, perhaps even a religious choice (*You see them in their Sunday clothes?*) to the voice on the other side, will it influence how you serve them? The patron has what is needed to be served right? Can you answer honestly?

I just wonder if we, as people professing to be Christians, have a choice in the way we serve. Can we know the worst about people and still serve them? You know, as Jesus did and still does? He knew then and knows now the messy parts of us but all He needs is your soul to serve you and serve you with eternal excellence.

My brother Christian had issues, a crazy past, pressing challenges that made his future look bleak to the natural eye, but he had a soul. He made many mistakes and, apparently, hurt many people, *but* he had what was needed if Jesus Christ were working the drive-thru, a *soul*. Christian may have had enemies, but nothing separated Him from the love God had for him because, he had a soul.

In conclusion, the spectrum of people served in a drive-thru is so wide, extremely diverse, and full of imperfections, but have one thing in common . . . a *soul*.

What if, just what if, Jesus worked the drive-thru?

Are you curious?

Date: _____

THE GREAT TRADE: MEMBERSHIP FOR FELLOWSHIP

MARCH 20, 2009

WOW! What a weekend!

I saw my crew! They are growing ridiculously fast! As you may know, I have asked you to pray for me as I consider leaving my crew with someone else after I am gone; the more they grow, the more I feel hesitant about doing so. My heart says to leave them to lead and keep each other accountable on their own because they enjoy the freedom experienced when together but I'll get back to this in a moment.

A couple of weeks ago, the Lord put it on my heart to start a Facebook group with my cousins . . . it has worked out well. I had been talking to God about how to get them, my crew, to connect heart-to-heart more, as I prepare them for my departure. We have been sharing some things that require transparency. I also shared with them about the Facebook group for my cousins, with the intent of challenging them to be a "living" Facebook. These young people were instructed to stay connected as a group with a different person leading the effort every week.

The first week went by with me not being able to see my crew due to a cancelation, but the second week, yesterday, we hooked up. I asked, "How did these two weeks go with staying connected?" They responded, "We made a group!" My response? "*Huh?* What group?" (Side bar: Most of the world has Facebook, my crew also has a type of Facebook. I knew that but didn't know groups could be created.) After realizing my students were listening to *every* word I had said when giving the example of a living Facebook, I asked, "Well do you have a name?"

The name of the group is, *The Family of Hope*! When they left my apartment, I ran, jumped, and screamed until I could not breathe, I was so excited! May I let you in on a lil' secret? I have been talking to the Lord about this, or should I say, He has been talking to me about this crew being my first "church plant," but I've been fighting with Him about it because I don't need what He has done to have a name for it to be legitimate. But God did it, reminding me of our discussion about my reluctance in claiming my first church plant. *This is it!* I love Him for it!

Please keep praying for us . . . It is my heart to find someone to host The Family of Hope when I am gone. I'm looking for someone to just give them a place to hang out once a week, to do what we've been doing, allowing God to lead.

P.S. JULY 25, 2018
This two-year teaching commitment started with these seven students and gave birth to "The Family of Hope." Looking back, this experience may have been water on the seed of my experience of fellowship while living in China. I was already experiencing fellowship but was a bit clueless to the fact. I was experiencing fellowship, for the first time, just amongst those I worked with, as we taught and loved our students. When my students came to me sharing their desire to give their collective gathering a name, the seed of fellowship rather than membership was watered.

The thing is, we hadn't learned anything about church membership. These kids, my students, wanted to name this gathering according to their experience and it was teaching me something new. Knowing only membership, the concept of fellowship was foreign to me and, as a matter of fact, I didn't know I'd never experienced fellowship all the years I was a member of several churches. Fellowship, by definition, is "a friendly association, especially with people who share one's interests." Words and phrases more closely associated to this new experience I was having are: companionship, companionability, sociability, comradeship, camaraderie, friendship, mutual support, togetherness, solidarity, informal, chumminess, "a community bound together in fellowship." Fellowship is and has always been meant for me to enjoy, evidenced by Genesis 2:18, as I believe, and it was my experience with several teaching partners and students.

To add, there was so much transparency accompanying the mutual support of these friendly, informal relationships. It was transformative! So much so that, I had to make the trade. I traded in membership (the fact of being a member of a group, the number or body of members in a group) for *fellowship*. This trade did not come without cost, but the truth and transparency I experience as part of relationships I now enjoy, was well worth the price of exchange. I am so grateful.

Are you curious?

Date: _____

WHO DO YOU SAY I AM?

APRIL 8, 2009

"When Jesus came into the coasts of Caesarea Philippi, he asked his disciples, saying, 'Whom do men say that I the Son of man am?' And they said, 'Some say that thou art John the Baptist: some, Elias; and others, Jeremiah's, or one of the prophets.' He said unto them, 'But whom say ye that I am?' And Simon Peter answered and said, 'Thou art the Christ, the Son of the living God.' And Jesus answered and said unto him, 'Blessed art thou, Simon Barjona: for flesh and blood hath not revealed it unto thee, but my Father which is in heaven. And I say also unto thee, That thou art Peter, and upon this rock I will build my church; and the gates of hell shall not prevail against it. And I will give unto thee the keys of the kingdom of heaven: and whatsoever thou shalt bind on earth shall be bound in heaven: and whatsoever thou shalt loose on earth shall be loosed in heaven.' Then charged he his disciples that they should tell no man that he was Jesus the Christ." (NIV)

What does it look like to "bind and loose?" I have prayed this having not been instructed, by Jesus, to do so. He doesn't tell Peter to pray it, declare it, proclaim it, speak it, etc. He just tells Peter this is going to be a reality for him. I asked this question of the text because as I was reviewing it, I heard one thing but was reading another: "God you said whatever we bind . . . and whatever we loose . . ." If we are going to quote God, that isn't what He said. And actually, Jesus said it to Peter. Could this have been personal prophecy to Peter? In this exchange Jesus changed Simon Barjona's name to Peter. Jesus told Peter he "would" give him the keys to the kingdom of heaven ("I will give . . ." When did that happen?), and then said, lastly, "what-soever you bind . . . loose."

Even after this observation, it can still be debated that this is a word to everybody who believes. Except, in my opinion, Jesus doesn't give us instructions on how to bind and loose. Was it a prophecy to Peter, but we were given the privilege of getting a glimpse into their relationship?

There are more questions where this one comes from. I've been going through this horrific stage in my relationship with God. I like to call it, "True, not true," or "What else have I been doing because it is popular?!" It is the worst to find out I have been walking on legs mostly made of tradition and religion. I am learning, for the first time, to walk out my relationship with God without the many "trappings" of tradition and religion. Being identified only by what cannot be seen is such a tight rope on which to balance. The fig leaves of religion gave me identity apart from God, you know, because fig leaves can be seen while He, on the other hand, cannot be.

P.S. JULY 16, 2018

As I continue my journey to freedom, more questions are revealed. However, this fig leaf stands out to me because it was my first questioning of things taught about the Bible, church, and religion that I exposed to someone else. I was reading this passage of scripture while reflecting on, hearing, and seeing the corporate declaration, "God, You said, 'Whatever we bind on earth, You will bind in heaven and whatever we loose on earth, You will loose in heaven.'" I'm watching Jesus give this permission, if you will, to Peter but remembering the "Whatever *we* . . ."

Does every word in the Bible belong to us all?

This prophecy to Peter was subsequent to a private conversation with his disciples and succeeded Jesus exposing his own sense of curiosity. Could Jesus's response to Peter's answer have been a personal promise? It seems many have read this, made this experience their own by reminding God, in prayer, of the passage. It's interesting to me that Christianity invites people to personal relationships with Jesus while it seems the personal relationships of Jesus's time are dismissed by the owning of many of their experiences.

Comparatively, this wasn't a major unveiling of uncommon questions, but it was a big deal, to me, to have revealed a question of this kind.

Are you curious?

Date: _____

HE'S A GOOD FRIEND

APRIL 12, 2009

What an awesome time with the crew today!

After discussing the reason Jesus is the most important stone and speaking about his forgiveness, one of the guys said, "Wow, he's a good friend." I could have cried! He followed up with, "I get nearer and nearer to him." My Bible students don't know the song "Nearer My God to Thee." After we finished praying, he said, "When I spoke to Him, I felt like He was standing right next to me."

You know, I thank God for friends and family, but I must agree, especially after these last couple of days, "He's a good friend." It's so refreshing and freeing to know that Jesus is the most important stone.

P.S. AUGUST 15, 2018

Reading this entry nine years later, I wonder if Jesus would have wanted me to highlight the importance of each of my students and the part they play in this world. I believe much of the message of Jesus Christ was to remind us of whom we've always been. Jesus reminded the multitudes of being the light of the world, the salt of the earth, a city on a hill, etc. He taught to love God with all of the heart, mind, and soul; to love their neighbors as they love themselves. I believe Jesus acknowledged the identity of those who would hear, and these acknowledgments were made before his death. Before there was the shedding of blood, Jesus acknowledged his audience as light and salt. Before he said, "It is finished," Jesus declared that it was already in us—a part of us—to love God and each other. Light, salt, and love wasn't something we had to *become* after Jesus Christ died, rose, and ascended. I believe Jesus was saying, "Light, salt, and love is who you are." Luke wrote in his book, "Now when He was asked by the Pharisees when the kingdom of God would come, He answered them and said, 'The kingdom of God does not come with observation;' nor will they say, 'See here!' or 'See there!' For indeed, the kingdom of God is within you." Jesus reminded even the most religious of them all, the Pharisees, that the kingdom of God was already in them.

While in China, I pointed my students to the significance of Jesus. But today, I am curious and contemplate the thought of pointing my students to their own quality of being, even as Jesus often did. Today, I contemplate the thought of Jesus giving his life for the *me* I'd always been, rather than my perceived inadequacies.

Freedom to contemplate . . .

Are you curious?

Date: _____

KNOWN BY WHAT CANNOT BE SEEN

SEPTEMBER 7, 2009

After spending two months in prayer and Bible reading during the holidays, the dust settled, and God began to speak to me about how I had been walking out my call to Him.

The Lord walked me through so much of what I believed to be truth—identifying untruthfulness, to which I'd committed. He called the untruth in my life *fig leaves.* He allowed me to see how much of who I was as a cover, a place to hide. The fig leaves were named: church membership, worship leader, minister, reverend, missionary, evangelist, "I'm a Christian," Just Come Ministries, "Chandrika Phea who takes her Bible wherever she goes," etc. In these roles and titles, my identity was found and behind them all, I hid.

As part of the "walk through," there was the uncovering of the fig leaves but not without explanation, questions, and further conversation. It was all exhausting, so much that I questioned God's very existence. After the experience, I felt naked. The only reality I could see was a question, "If I am not those assigned roles and titles, *who am I?*"

It was time to learn how to walk out my call to God absent of the fig leaves.

The question, "Can you be identified only by what cannot be seen?" solidified a space at the foundation of self-discovery going forward.

P.S. NOVEMBER 11, 2018

Behind the label of "preacher's kid," behind the ministerial title, worship leader, preacher, reverend, Christian, was a shoplifter. The Bibles I preached sermons from had been shoplifted (personally monogrammed). The worship music I presented to congregations was from CDs I'd stolen off the shelves of the stores distributing them. Right beyond the fig leaves was a liar, a girl who believed all of these titles had a specific look and style, and I went to ridiculous extents to look the part. Under these fig leaves, I only knew who I was by what I was told I'd be, a church leader. I knew nothing of myself beyond all of the greenery, beyond all of the trappings.

When I moved to China, none of these titles existed. *Now what? Who am I now? What, now, is there to do?*

Carrying my Bible everywhere, as I'd been "known for" in the states, wasn't an option in China. The "God's got your back" jacket I wore attracted the attention of those who believed my reason for being in the Asian country was to begin an underground Christian church. The proud church member I once was ceased to be an option while living abroad.

This two-year commitment was the beginning of learning who I was not.

Let the journey continue . . .

Are you curious?

Date: _____

FOR AN UNBORN GENERATION

MARCH 19, 2010

[23]For I received from the Lord what I also passed on to you: The Lord Jesus, on the night was betrayed, took bread, [24]and when had given thanks, he broke it and *said*, "This is my body, which is for you; do this in remembrance of me." [25]In the same way, after supper he took the cup, *saying*, "This cup is the new covenant in my blood; do this, whenever you drink it, in remembrance of me." [26]For whenever you eat this bread and drink this cup, you proclaim the Lord's death until he comes.—1 Cor. 11:23-26

[19]And he took bread, gave thanks and broke it, and gave it to them, *saying*, "This is my body given for you; do this in remembrance of me."

[20]In the same way, after the supper he took the cup, *saying*, "This cup is the new covenant in my blood, which is poured out for you. [21]But the hand of him who is going to betray me is with mine on the table. [22]The Son of Man will go as it has been decreed, but woe to that man who betrays him."—Luke 22:19-22[2]

The way in which these verses were written, Paul seems to have been quoting Jesus. However, it wasn't recorded of Jesus to have said, "whenever you drink it" or "*as oft as you drink it*," which is used to validate the implementation of what has now become a repetitive ceremony. Introduced by the words "said" or "saying," this set of scriptures, in many versions of the Bible, are printed in red ink to differentiate the voice of Jesus from other voices of his time. John seemed to focus on other parts of the experience. Matthew and Mark stop short of "do this in

---

2 I have chosen to emphasize in italics the words and phrases from this passage which I find to be exceptionally important.

remembrance of me," in their recalling of the experience. And let's not talk about all of the verses Paul wrote following the quotation marked verses. The Last Supper, The Lord's Supper, Eucharist, Holy Communion, Communion, Sacrament of the Table, Blessed Sacrament, all seem to come from man's interpretation of that time Jesus had with the disciples. According to John, Jesus, after his resurrection, reunited with the disciples and enjoyed breakfast with them. Why hasn't that moment been titled and replicated? I believe if others, absent of the experience, took the freedom to interpret the meal before the last meal Jesus enjoyed with the disciples, it is okay for me to take the freedom not to interpret the same.

Can we start over? I don't know how to start again without going back to find out how we, in general, got *here* in the first place. By here, I mean the place we are in after decades and decades of religion.

For the sake of an unborn generation, I am exploring.

P.S. DECEMBER 16, 2018

Sharing what I'd call inconsistencies regarding Communion pales in comparison to how tough it was reading Matthew, Mark, and Luke's account of Jesus's last Passover with his apostles. Reading through the eyes and experience of God's love, rather than through the religious experience of Communion, left me with mixed emotions: angry then joyful. Growing up in Pentecostal church, this Communion experience looked so different from what I was reading for myself. It became difficult to understand why people identify themselves apart from each other in their participation of the ceremony. Pastors who are on raised platforms behind podiums, deaconesses in their uniforms, missionaries, associate pastors, "church mothers," lay members, all wore clothing communicating differences from the others. There were specific roles that earned the privilege of leading this commemoration. One role was holding the plates containing bread and grape juice and the other was standing in front of the congregation as congregants waited their turn. In some cases, children weren't allowed to participate because this ceremony involved a level of sacredness that could only be understood by the most mature in the room. But to read Jesus's last Passover with his apostles, apart from the ritual reading of 1 Corinthians 11:23-26 during the Communion ceremony, was distinctively different from what I'd observed most of my life.

The Gospel passages don't read of Jesus standing at an elevated space and place. There was no podium, no pulpit. His invitation didn't, in its very essence, resemble what was written in the first Corinthian letter, i.e., verses 26-30. As a matter of fact, The New International Version of the Bible reads in Luke 22:14 that Jesus and his apostles "reclined at the table." The use of the word reclined is actually "to lay." Jesus wasn't wearing an exclusively elongated vestment. *What about a clergy collar? Where was his staff? Where was his assistant to help crown his head with a significantly jeweled headpiece?*

Luke, in his book, writes of Jesus this; "And he said unto to them, 'I have eagerly desired to eat this Passover with you before I suffer. For I tell you, that I will not eat it again until it finds fulfillment in the kingdom of God.'" I believe when Jesus told the disciples to "Do this in remembrance of me," he had in mind that it would be his last opportunity to participate in such fellowship with them.

How did this experience of casual fellowship, relationship, and love, become a repetitive monthly ceremony remembering the eminent death of Jesus, full of grandiose expression, cloaked with "For as often as you do this. . . ?"

For generations to come, I ask.

Are you curious?

Date: _____

THE MEDITATION OF MY HEART

JANUARY 29, 2010

If my perspective (the way in which objects appear to the eye or one's point of view) is of this world, the supernatural is very much a reality. If I have an eternal perspective, an eternal seat with God, what is considered supernatural here on earth would just be natural or normal from my seat with Him.

P.S. DECEMBER 20, 2018

The shedding of religion, or fig leaves, as I call it, had become quite regular. I started to think and perceive from an unlimited place of existence, thoughts—beyond restriction. The more of Christianity I shed, the more I imagine existing in and from a place where the concept of needs isn't real. While submitting to the act of shedding religion, a whole new version of me was beginning to be revealed. This envisioning became a constant practice and God offered language for what was being revealed in this *high place*. Are miracles needed in this place? Does one's body need to be healed in this location? Is there a devil to fight up this high? Even the necessity of faith became questionable in this new space. Just as I asked many questions of my realtor while she presented options for new places of residence, in this new locale, from this new perspective, though invisible, I am asking questions about all I've known for so many years.

Are you curious?

Date: _____

SEEING IS CHANGING

MARCH 23, 2010

"In this world you don't have to ask," is contrary to "*Ask* and it shall be . . . ," "If you *ask* in my name . . . ," ". . . you *ask* amiss," "I know what you need before you *ask*," "*Ask* what you will and it shall be done. . . ," "Now this is the confidence that we have in Him, that if we *ask* anything according to His will, He hears us. And if we know that He hears us, whatever we *ask*, we know that we have the petitions that we have *asked* of Him," etc.

I closed my eyes to another place of existence as God stood next to me introducing me to another truth pertaining to where we were in that moment. He said, "Here, you don't have to ask." I tried staying on my knees to pray like I'd always done but there was nothing to do, nothing to say. This is only one example of stepping out to walk in the direction of what's not written, of what "cannot be confirmed Biblically." I loved it! It changed the way I pray almost immediately after reminding God of the Bible verses stating the opposite. "I know, but in this world, you don't have to ask," He said again.

The more I see of God, the more things change. How do I see more of Him but continue with some of the same beliefs and practices?

P.S. JANUARY 14, 2019

This experience left me desiring to be more polite in my relationship with God, if you will. What else is there to offer in a place where needs are non-existent? All there was to be was grateful, not for the experience alone but for what the experience *meant* for my life. I got on my knees to pray, closed my eyes, only to see I was in another world. Yes, it sounds crazy, but it was a vision, of sorts. In this world introduced to me, there was no such thing as a "need." Everything was there, including the voice of God talking to me as though He knew what my prayers would consist of. There was such a sense of completeness in this world and in me. If the wind was present, it felt like it was blowing through me, keeping me full, almost to the point of tears. How would I, could I, after such an experience, go back to the same type of exchanges with God? How could I return to what I'd always known as prayer? How could I continue to *ask* of God . . . *plead* with God, for what I believed I needed?

There are a few scriptures I could refer to, validifying my experience and how it changed me, but confidently, those verses weren't needed. It was too late; this vision, this experience, changed me . . . forever.

Seeing as I did was transformative. The experience altered me and overwhelmed my perspective of what I had believed to be my reality before the vision.

Seeing is changing. Going back to what I'd always known, would be to dishonor God's love for me in showing me something different.

Forever changed.

Are you curious?

Date: _____

DOES THE WIND EVER STOP BLOWING UP THAT HIGH?

AUGUST 19, 2010

After doing some research, can I assume it doesn't? Is it okay to admit not being able to fathom the wind not always blowing when you are off the ground?

This question led me to another. Why go through all the trouble of jumping out of a plane, releasing the parachute, soaring, then asking for wind? To be *in* the wind but still *ask* for it, speaks to having the wrong perspective, wouldn't you say?

Another question comes to mind; Why ask, beg, or plead for a glory we already have, a glory we already live in? It's like asking, begging, or pleading for the wind that is already carrying you. God asked me, "If you sit in heavenly places, as a believer, why ask for what you have access to?" It would seem the wind would just allow me to *be*.

I won't ask God anymore that His glory "fill this place." In my world, His glory is this place. When up high, in heavenly places, God's permanent existence is the glory we seek. It is from the high place, that perspective, I can see the earth below, filled with His glory. When up that high, in the heavenly places, you don't have to ask for a visitation from Jesus, right? Just look over to the place of endlessness, there, you will *find* him . . . look behind you, where no beginning can be found, and you will *see* him. The difference between a physical flight and where God made us to sit, is the lack of gravity. Our residence is "up that high." This perspective allows me to just *be*. I don't have to "go in," "come out," "prepare my heart for." Up that high, I have the eternal Word. Up that high, all my prophecies are fulfilled.

Where the wind never stops blowing, I don't have to ask for a greater anointing. I can rest, be, live. Up where the wind never stops blowing, I imagine the wind that carries me is what clothes me. No need to be identified by anything other than wind.

I believe, for those in relationship with God, this and so much more, is our reality . . . up that high.

P.S. JANUARY 8, 2019

I had a chance to watch an acquaintance skydive. I'd seen skydivers before, but this diver was the first whom I knew personally. Later that night, as I lie down for bed, God brought it back to me with all the questions shared in this journal entry.

These questions reflect where I was in my life of prayer, particularly, relating to corporate gatherings for prayer. My limit of spending time in prayer with others devoting much of that allotment to begging and pleading for the presence that is God had been reached. I know, just as the prior entry reads and reminds us, there is scripture suggesting we ask for what we want and for what we need.

Asking, begging, and pleading seems to contradict the position my spiritual reality occupies. Wouldn't believing I sit in heavenly places make tangible the statement, "But God will supply all my needs according to his riches in Glory by Christ Jesus?" And I'd even go further to challenge this declaration in Paul's letter to Philippi by asking him, "If I sit in heavenly places, what needs do I have for God to supply?"

I'd offer to Paul, the apostle, that sitting in a place of provision while expecting "God will supply" is like skydiving from a plane, begging and pleading not to be dropped, all while the wind fills the attached parachute, carrying its diver.

The wind is carrying us. Just be. Just live and live abundantly, "Up that High."

Are you curious?

Date: _____

ANDRE'S QUESTION

SEPTEMBER 7, 2010

"Why do you go to church?" he asked.

When asked the question, the only answer I had was the only answer I knew. It was the only answer to the question I'd been taught: "Not forsaking the assembling of ourselves together, as the manner of some is; but exhorting one another: and so much the more, as ye see the day approaching," Hebrews 10:25. But suddenly, that answer wasn't enough anymore. How could it be enough after spending two years away from the ritual of going to church?

This question moved me to look again at the Hebrews verse only to find it has nothing to do with what has *become* church, nothing to do with Bible study on Wednesday night, weekly seasonal revivals, conferences, etc. Most often, we in Western religious culture read that Bible verse through the eyes of our own experiences from which our perspectives have been derived. When we have read, heard, and been taught this verse for generations before us, it has been interpreted as "going to church."

After studying the word "church" in its original language, I learned it is not an activity. I have never forgotten going to a Christian gathering once and asking God, "Why is the use of this word as some *place* to go annoying me today?" He answers back with this reminder and more, "You've heard people say, Church is not an organization it's an organism. Church is an existence." I went back to one of the first places the word is used and replaced the word *church* with *existence*, "Upon this rock I will build my *existence* and the gates of hell shall not prevail against my *existence* (it)." The exclamation, "Ooooweee! We had church!" has become a very intriguing sentiment to me. Church is not anything to be had. Our fellowship around what we have in common may come to an end, but *church* is never over. The word existence means the state of existing; of being. In other words, church is not something to *do*, it is something to *be*. If we, "the church", became half of what we do, I believe we could change the world at a faster pace! That rocked me, especially the part about hell not prevailing against the existence of Christ (in the Earth, in you, in me). The word church is translated from "Ekklesia." It means "a calling out." If you are called out, and only God knows, you are the church.

I believe we, in general, have been missing God and experiences with Him because the congregation is limited to what is seen as the "assembling of yourselves." If you are married to a man who is a believer and you guys sit at the dining room table, is that not "Where two or three gather in my name, there I am in the midst?" However, I'd argue that when you and a best girlfriend are hanging out, not talking about Jesus, but both love God and love to shop, that it is pleasing to God.

I also speak of my own experience. I lived in China for two years where church is not celebrated, but breakfast with my friends and teammates was communion. We were brothers and sisters having one thing in common, living in China to love our students . . . God smiles. We are the existence of God on the Earth, the Ekklesia. We are a congregation and in us lies a generation that will be and is loved by our Father.

I'll end with this quote; "Preach the gospel at all times. Use words only when necessary," St. Francis of Assisi.

Be what you *Believe*.

P.S. JANUARY 3, 2019

Andre, a man after God's heart, is how I'd describe this guy I met in China while we worked at the same university. This is a man whose heart to please God in every way, a very sincere worshipper and worship leader. What? You thought an atheist presented that question to me? No. This is a part of what makes this question so significant. To add, let's cover a few questions not asked in this exchange:

1. What does the Bible say about going to church?
2. What were you taught about going to church?

Since the question posed was, "Why do *you* go to church?" I had to take a moment to really think my answer through. I needed to search my thoughts, search my heart.

Where I landed is that a "calling out" is something to be rather than a "place to go to." It is a participating *as* not a participating *in*.

I can't even begin to imagine how many Chinese citizens I'd walk by, daily, who are in relationship with God. For so long, Western Christians have seen the Chinese lack of freedom to worship openly as a hindrance to their society. But I see the religious restrictions of China as a gift. The thing is, they must *be* what they believe. The Chinese citizens of Asia who are in relationship with God can't wear it, join it, advertise with a bumper sticker on their vehicles, or carry a Bible everywhere. It could lead to their persecution; all the things westerners get to do to identify ourselves according to our religious belief. Does the experience of ecclesiastical restraint make the Chinese believer any less committed to their relationships with God? Surely not. Their commitment to our God must look like what Jesus said to his disciples, "By this all men will know that you are disciples, if you love one another." They must be known only by the love they have for each other.

Andre's question set me on a new journey to participating as rather than participating in.

There is a becoming of the "love one another" and that becoming redirected my life's pursuit.

I am grateful, Andre, for your presence in my life and your question.

Are you curious?

Date: _____

BY DEFINITION

Rebel, a person who refuses allegiance to, resists, or rises in arms against the government or ruler of his or her country/to resist or rise against some authority, control, or tradition.

Jesus Christ was a rebel, in my opinion. There may be some who'd disagree, but we would not be free from our sins had he, Christ, not rebelled against the religious world of his time. They would not have killed Christ except that he rebelled against their rules, traditions, regulations, etc. He came to show us a more excellent way.

Many faiths (denominations) of our day have adopted traditions and beliefs, if you will, from what is known as the Protestant church. Martin Luther? He rebelled against the Roman Catholic Church, of which was later called, "The Protestant Reformation."

Martin Luther King was a rebel, or that of the rebellious kind. If it weren't for his, and many others, rebelling against the "ruler of his/our country," it might be a while longer before the desegregation of schools, voting restrictions of Black people, cotton picking, and water fountains labeled "nigger" would be done away with.

Rosa Parks? A rebel. Rosa's refusal to give up a front seat on the bus she was riding sparked an entire bus boycott because of her "rise against some authority." We would not have had any idea of the Underground Railroad if it weren't for rebellion, the rebellious, or rebels.

This is near and dear to my heart because I've been called a rebel. Without hesitation, I've been told, "You are rebellious." I no longer surrender to the negative intent of such a label. I feared the word to be altogether negative, an evil I was possessed with, until I simply looked at the definition. The meaning of the word is a reminder that many of the freedoms enjoyed today are because someone was rebellious—a rebel.

The previous list is neck-deep in legendary status; people who have set standards that won't be forgotten for ages to come. It's a compliment and I'm honored to be ranked among the greats! Some of these same greats, especially Jesus Christ, inspire and remind me I am not alone.

More often than not, it takes a rebel to change the world around us.

P.S. JANUARY 15, 2019

In recent years, I have come to believe it takes one who does not possess courage to label the courage of others as "a spirit of rebellion"—a spirit needing to be purged, in their opinion. Most often, those who lack courage *admire* the courageous. Rather than seeking to be audacious, it is easier to rebuke and cast out what is really the audacity of another.

I am a rebel.

Are you curious?

Date: _____

CULTURE SHOCK

JULY 21, 2011

Three years ago, Father's Day, I experienced culture shock for the first time in my life. I lived in China almost a year but never experienced that type of anxiety.

I was standing in the corner of the youth room of a church the first time I experienced culture shock. The very common exclamations, "The devil is crazy," "the enemy in your life," traveled through the sound system filling the room. My eyes got big! For the first time in an entire year, I was hearing such things and having not heard these words in so long was scary!

Because of this confusion, upon my return to China for a second year of teaching, I committed to further study of the subjects contributing to the experience of shock. I came to a place of deciding to believe that "the enemy in my life" is defeated and had been since God said, "the woman will give birth to a seed who will crush the head of the serpent."

But what further antagonized me was that I lived in a building of about ninety-nine percent believers but hadn't heard much church jargon, if at all. "Why aren't I hearing the devil mentioned at all?" God pointed to the difference between cultures of individuals living in the building. I was a part of the minority and it appears the steadfast celebration of the devil may be cultural.

I've asked myself, "What if it's true, that the seed of the woman crushed the head of serpent (devil)? What if Jesus took the keys of death, hell, and the grave? What if what Jesus said about the prince of this world being condemned is true? What if when Jesus said, 'It is finished,' it really was finished? Then who or what would be to blame?" Me. I am no longer afraid of taking responsibility for my own actions.

After coming to believe much of what was written in the gospels, I wouldn't be afraid to ask James, who wrote the instruction to resist the devil, "How do you resist a defeated devil?"

P.S. JANUARY 17, 2019

In short, among other things, I decided to resign fighting with a defeated devil.

Before going to live in China, I'd never left the country. It was expected and even a part of training to prepare for culture shock in the first few weeks of our arrival to the ancient Asian country. The preparation made me anxious since so much weight was placed on missing family and western conveniences. We landed in Shanghai and then were driven to the university where we would become instructors. We then moved into our apartments. Our first week came and went, then the second week, the first month, six months. Months passed, being full of a new and vibrant reality, but never did I experience the expected culture shock as a part of it all.

An entire school year went by, and it was time to head back to the States for the summer, though I signed a contract to return to China for another year of teaching at summer's end. I returned to America with a plan to see the many faces I loved and missed. One of the places I was certain to see the most faces at once, was the church I attended before my adventure to China. I dressed in the required attire, got in my car, and headed to join this Sunday morning gathering of people. I entered the building and found a seat closest to a wall. As per the norm, prayer began, the worship leaders took their places, and everyone focused in on their reason for being in the room. The further we got into our reason for being there, the more I started to hear what I had not heard for the entire year abroad. It was literally culture shock to hear, "The devil is crazy . . .", "the enemy in your life . . .", "Let's prepare are hearts for Communion", "Who needs an offering envelope?" The gathering of offering envelopes to be passed out to participants had a deafening sound. I was in complete shock and never had I experienced such a thing.

The shock wasn't that I'd not heard these phrases or participated in these rituals for a year. The shock came from living a full year, in another country, never *realizing* my life was absent of these reminders and ordnances.

Subsequent to this experience of culture shock, I was left asking God, "Why? Why have I not been aware of these absences? Am I going to hell because I lived a year without talking about the devil? What does it mean not to have taken Communion in a year? Why have I experienced Your provision in my life like never before but haven't tithed or given an offering in almost twelve months? If I've not been participating in these traditions, what have I been doing?"

The culture shock and questions asked as a result of this religious jarring led me on a journey that gave cause for deep examination of my closely guarded beliefs. Much like a forensic examiner, I grabbed my shovel and committed to the exhumation and investigation of my doctrinal convictions.

Are you curious?

Date: _____

THE BEGINNING AND END OF GOD

JANUARY 11, 2012
How can a God, of whom we say has no beginning and no end, be contained in a book, having a beginning and an end?

P.S. JANUARY 24, 2019
I was teased for choosing to stay in my university apartment during the middle of winter in Central China just to read my Bible every day until I exhausted every verse. From my neighbors, I collected as many space heaters as were available because controlling the temperature in my residence wasn't an option since there was no thermostat. Most of my partners in love and education traveled to Asia's warmer areas, leaving a very few of us to survive the expected brutal chill during that time of year.

Every morning, for two-and-a-half months, I'd awake to grab breakfast, fellowship with those of us taking advantage of an almost empty cafeteria, then head back up to my apartment. Every day was new because I'd committed to reading and completing at least one book of the Bible within those twenty-four hours. All I needed to consistently keep this promise to myself was setup. Bible, *check*. Heaters, *check*. Blanket, *check*. Bible on CD, *check*. Yes!

A beautiful couple blessed me with *The Bible Experience*. It was purchased to assist my students in their learning of the English language and to help them spiritually even while growing in my native tongue. However, I used the set of CDs to keep me on course in accomplishing my goal.

I remember feeling a bit overwhelmed when opening my red hardcover, *The Knowing Jesus Study Bible*, the New International

Version, wondering if I'd finish what I set out to do. But there I went. I pressed the play button on the CD player and heard, "In the beginning God . . ." as I made sure to read every word, whether I knew them or not.

But just as overwhelmed as I was when opening this book, I was overwhelmed at the closing of it, literally. I was angry and happy, confused and clear, full and empty. My emotions were all over the place.

There were a few questions I asked of God and there were answers. But the first statement I heard from God after closing the book was, "Now that you have studied everyone else's experience of me, I am ready to give you your own."

God has done just that. One of those experiences is never ending. It is the experience of an unchangeable completeness, a completeness experienced beyond the beginning and the end of the Bible. The fullness I began to experience after the opening and closing of the book was something I don't recall reading. Of course, this kind of measureless abundance is written of and it is even promised but reading any personal experiences of this kind escapes me.

This reality of completeness doesn't seem to have a Genesis. This reality is void of an "In the beginning." An introduction can't be found because it seems to have always been–this place of completeness. There is no opening or close of it, as I had opened and closed my Bible, day after day. There is no end to it, even as I read the last word, "Amen." This reality of completeness doesn't have an origin, while the history of Christianity can be traced back to its start. This reality of completeness, unlike the Bible, has no inception. This experience, gifted to me by God, expands beyond the cover, the stitch, the ink, and pages of the two biblical Testaments.

How? How can God and my *experience* of Him, be restricted to a book having a beginning and end? How can God and my experience of Him be restricted to the experiences of those who wrote as a result of their own?

I refuse the notion, of which I've heard for years, "If it isn't in the Bible, it isn't God."

There are so many scriptures to offer, validating my consistent experience of God but simply put, if it must be written in the Bible for it to be God, it isn't God we read of in its books.

Are you curious?

Date: _____

PAUL SAID!

If I have questions, surely Paul did, right?

Paul, the apostle, is a writer of many of the New Testament books. As a matter of fact, thirteen or more books of the NT are attributed to Paul but only seven of them are believed to be authentically dictated by him.

Come with me. Yes, you. Come. I want to go see Paul and I don't want to go alone. Are you coming?

Let's visit Paul, the apostle, in our imagination.

We have arrived. Do you see him? Paul? Do ya?

Well, what do you see? What is your first observation of him?

My first observation of Paul is that he's actually a human being. Even if one believes this whole Bible thing to be a big sham, its stories and letters still involve the thought of human beings interacting with a God they believed in.

Paul, according to his personal story authored by Luke, was born Saul. This formally instructed Pharisee went through a name change but prior to the experience leading to an identity shift, Paul was a self-proclaimed persecutor of the church, blasphemer, nonbeliever, and a sinner. He was on the road, traveling to another city, with a permission slip, collecting and imprisoning those who were of *The Way*. While traveling to Damascus, Saul believed he encountered and was confronted by Jesus in a vision that left him blind. The men with the now visionless persecutor led him to Damascus by hand, where the disability continued for three days. Through a series of events thereafter, Saul's sight was fully restored, then he was baptized. While spending some time with the disciples in the area, Saul began to preach in the synagogues as a result of his new revelation. Snagged and escorted to Antioch, Saul joined Barnabas to teach disciples there. This was the beginning of Saul's new journey, introducing Jesus to the Gentiles. It is believed he went on to plant fourteen to twenty churches.

Now that Paul has made his acquaintance, we know he is mortal, as we are, by recalling what was written of his journey. Let's assume that along the way, this apostle asked questions. If he did ask questions, let's assume he asked God questions. I do; do you? Do you ask questions? Do you ask God questions? If I ask questions of God and you ask questions of God, surely Paul did. He experienced such an abrupt and impactful transformation; how could he not have had an untrained curiosity? He had only known the law of Moses and the Jewish (Hebrew) culture in which he was reared. This until, he had seen, what Luke referred to as, "a light," and now had the assignment of introducing that light to a people who had been excluded from that teaching.

Did Paul ask God questions? Surely.

Since we have established that Paul probably lacked an inherent wisdom on every subject presented to him on this new mission, let's assume a third of his writings, a half, a tiny fragment read of this missionary's letters to the believers in these cities, are a result of questions he asked God.

All of the aforementioned led me to share my own questions: Did Paul ask every question? (Feel free to answer aloud). My answer is a resounding, "No." I ask another question: If Paul didn't ask every question, did he have every answer? Again, I offer, a resounding, "No." This resolve led me to an additional question: If Paul didn't ask every question, did he have and write every answer in these letters?

My sense of curiosity has been resurrected and it took moving to another country to experience its restoration. It took relocating to learn God had never asked me to trade my

intellectual inquisitiveness about life and relationship with
Him for the salvation Christianity offered.

An appreciation can be found for much of what Paul said
but, I have been given the gift of spiritual curiosity, if you will,
and I imagine it'll take the rest of my life to unwrap it.

Are you curious?

Date: _____

MY FIRST VISIT TO A JEWISH SYNAGOGUE

MARCH 14, 2012

I visited the Jewish Synagogue on Sunday, the one across from my apartment complex.

What an experience and one unlike anything I expected. I met Ronnett and Jeffrey (the Rabbi), and shared with them my heart for the community I live in. "I have wanted to bring my apartment community, across the street, together for some time now. Would you guys help me do that? As a part of our community and we a part of your community?" I asked. The two of them seemed a bit confused by my inquiry, saying, "You do know that this is a synagogue, right?" I shared further, "I know some of the people who live in my community, and I'd like to have some kind of BBQ, picnic, or something that would bring us all together to meet one another."

Jeffery explained that their synagogue doesn't "do apartment complexes."

Ronnett proceeded to show me around but, while headed to the library, she asked, "You do know this is a Jewish Library, right?" She goes on to explain Easter is coming up and with Christians believing Jews killed Jesus, their Jewish community was on edge. I had no idea Jews felt as though they still had a reason to fear. At one point, she exclaimed, "I would love for everybody to be a Jew!"

"Ma'am? I don't want to be a Jew and neither do I want to be a Christian. I just want to love God and love people. Jesus told us to love our neighbor as we love ourselves. He didn't say, 'Love your neighbor only if they are Christian, only if they are Jewish, straight, gay, young, old, republican, democrat, white, black, or only when there is agreement.' There was no classification given. I just desire to meet, learn, and love my neighbors. You guys are my neighbors. From my perspective, before you are a Jew, you are my neighbor," I offered. Needless to say, Ronnett was shocked.

She said, "We are in the Bible belt. People don't say that kind of thing."

Being a bit overwhelmed, I found a seat. Ronnett exited, and I was left in the library with a lady who'd listened to the entire exchange. I asked her a question or two, but she in turn said to me, "It sounds like you are on an amazing journey, and I am ready to go on it with you."

Ya' know, going to the synagogue intending to learn was the goal but it seems as though we all learned something.

Jeremiah believed God spoke to him and said, "Before I formed you in the belly, I knew you." I am conflicted in believing the me God knew before forming me in the belly was that of a Christian. It is through this sense of confliction that I see the same of other religions.

P.S. FEBRUARY 21, 2019

Almost immediately, after returning to the States from China, the process of learning who I was *not*, began. It was and still can be likened to the stripping away of fig leaves.

Imagine that.

Imagine the voice of God looking for Adam, finding him clothed in fig leaves. What if, when asked, "Who told you that you were naked?" Adam defrocked himself of what covered his new personal perception?

It was about three months into my China residency that I realized my minister's license meant nothing. The crucifix I wore, ever so faithfully, only attracted the attention of those who oppose what they believed it represented, Christianity. My jacket of choice had stitched on it, "God's Got Your Back." Back home, a few of my friends wrote a song about me carrying a Bible everywhere. The song was true to form. Never did I leave my house, my vehicle even, without a Bible in hand. Living out the lyrics of such an endearing anthem while in Asia would have caused more of a headache than could have been afforded. But as time went on, the symbolism used to identify me apart from those I was there to serve, became less and less significant. It all meant nothing.

The nothing that all of the fig leaves meant, left me feeling bare and even more questions came of feeling stripped. If in China my credentials held no weight and if these external classifications only caused trouble, then who was I without them? I couldn't wear a crucifix comfortably, couldn't carry a Bible, and my favorite jacket drew undesired attention. How do I now identify as a Christian?

Pause.

Is who I am a Christian?

Does God see me as a Christian?

If God knew me before forming me in the womb, as the prophet Jeremiah wrote of his own experience, did He know me as a Christian?

I often daydream about what in life is being missed due to so many external allowances for identifying us apart from the other.

Did God know us as Jews before we were formed in the womb?

Did God know us as Baptist or Methodist Christians before we were formed in the womb?

Did God know us as Catholics, Muslims, or Hindus before we were formed in the womb?

Time away from the culture supporting my fig leaves allowed me to see them, these leaves of cover, and ask of them, questions. As it seems, the answer to my questions have a perpetual answer; this endless curiosity will forever offer something new to learn.

Are you curious?

Date: _____

THE BIBLE DOES NOT CONTRADICT ITSELF

MAY 13, 2012

I, too, adopted the thought of scripture contradicting itself. Then, I read the entire Bible—page by page, book by book.

Bible, the meaning of the word derived from the Greek word "biblia" meaning "the books" or "biblion" meaning "book." It was after reading the entire Bible that I was inspired to investigate Bible as a word. I, one who graduated from a Bible University with a Biblical Studies Degree, looked into the definition of the word itself, having never done so before.

To learn that I'd read this Bible as the book it is, blew my mind. Why wouldn't it surprise me? I'd never read it as a book before. I'd been reading applicable scriptures for the moment, breaking them down word for word as it related to the original languages in which they were written. Not only was I cheating myself but cheating the authors and the God they wrote about.

Christianity teaches there is no beginning and no end to the God fueling its movement. The Christian religion also declares God as omnipresent—being present everywhere at the same time. As is taught, this God is a reality to be experienced of which can't be traced back to an origin, a God who will never die, who is ever-present with the capability to have and manage a relationship with every human He created.

If the God of Christianity is even bigger than what is described in the aforementioned paragraph, why wouldn't there be an experience of this deity designated just for me? God? Who has no beginning and no end?

Pause.

Heard of the Red Sea opening for anyone else?

How about a burning bush, unconsumed by the flames, talking to a man? Has anyone else experienced a contained fiery orating hedge? *No?*

What about a guy being swallowed by a whale? Did anyone else have that experience?

A prophet taken up to heaven in a chariot.

A guy on his way to another city, mounting the back of a beast, but never arriving to the desired place to persecute believers because of a light coming out of the sky that blinded him and changed his life forever.

I choose to believe in the immeasurable nature of who God is, but if this is the case, if it is that I am experiencing an unmeasurable God, there has to be an experience of His reality designated just for me. Surely there is an experience of His presence that is unique to my existence on this planet.

There is an experience of God assigned to me alone and while choosing to believe this, I have to believe the same of those who wrote of their experiences included in this book called "Bible."

Coming to accept that everyone's experience of God is going to be different, has been extremely liberating. We as humans, while experiencing all God is to us, are responsible for interpreting such inward phenomena. Our very personal interpretations of our very personal experiences of the same Spirit that is God, will be different. A contradiction? No. Different? Of course. Assuredly, it is the same of those who have lived before us, including the authors of what is known as the bestselling book in the world.

If there can be no difference between our personal experiences and interpretations of divinity, it isn't God that we are experiencing.

Are you curious?

Date: _____

ACCESS DENIED

NOVEMBER 20, 2012
But the image and likeness remain.

The Bible opens up with a book called Genesis, believed to be authored by Moses. The word Genesis is defined as "the origin."

As I am reading the first two chapters of The Beginning, apparently it is with an unconscious expectation. I am, without intent, looking for Adam and Eve to eat of the Tree of the Knowledge of Good and Evil, God looking for Adam, Adam informing God of the part his wife played in what he'd been instructed *not* to do, and both of them being told to leave the Garden, leading to their ultimate separation from God.

With the incognizant expectancy to read what I'd been taught, I found myself flipping through those first three chapters looking for where God separated Himself from His creation. But I couldn't find that which I'd been taught.

The practice of going to the place of my reading, became easier to do over time, almost habitual. Like a preschooler at story time, I went there, I sat, crossed one leg over the other, and watched each word play out as much as was possible.

I watched God, after His instructions not to eat of the tree was evaded by this couple, curse the serpent. My observation of Eve continued as God laid out the consequences of her actions. I sat attentively as the particulars of Adam's consequence were handed to him. After which, there was a dismal of the two.

We don't read that Adam and Eve got to the exit of their inherited residence only for God to, lastly, demand of them to, "leave my image at the door before you go."

Access to the garden was denied but God didn't take His image and likeness back.

Where is the separation from our omnipresent God?

If the image and likeness of God we were created in, was not lost, what *was* lost?

Are you curious?

Date: _____

RELIGION: MY DEFINITION

JANUARY 14, 2013

What if religion is the process and practice of identifying one-self apart from another? What if the process and practice of identifying oneself apart from another is the practice and process of identifying oneself from the image and likeness of God?

These questions are derived from the concept of "Lord make me over, "There's nobody like you," ". . . create a better me." The constant identifying ourselves apart from our Creator, to worship Him, is embedded in the lyrics of many songs assigned to Christianity. But perceiving ourselves apart from God, of whose likeness we bear, most likely contributes to seeing ourselves apart from our neighbors, i.e., my definition of religion.

P.S. NOVEMBER 3, 2018

As I see it, religion is the need to be identified apart from another person or group. It is the effort, the energy spent, separating oneself from that which is its same. Religion is the clothing, perhaps, the fig leaves of *doing* difference.

In the Book of Genesis, Moses writes that God asked Adam, "Who told you that you were naked?" It seems the sentiment of the question was that of, "Who told you that you were different from me?"

In my estimation, religion is the refusal to see our neighbor as ourselves.

God asked a question of Adam and I ask the same of us, *"Who told us we were different from each other?"*

Are you curious?

Date: _____

IDENTIFIED BY LOVE

JANUARY 20, 2013

It is written, "By this everyone will know that you are my disciple, if you love one another."

Simply put, be identified by love.

Jesus didn't say his disciples would be known by the Bible they carry, denomination/organized religion they've joined. To be known by the love you have for another is to be identified by it, love. To be identified by love is to BE God because, as it is written, God is Love.

Still learning . . .

P.S. MAY 1, 2019

"Still learning . . ." about God, the presence of God in my life, and His image expressed as *me*. I spent two years in China teaching a Bible study to seven freshman college students while teaching oral English communication to many of their peers. Praying about where to start, I believed the Gospels would be the best place, the book of Luke being the specific text to complete, and it took all of the two years of my residency to do so. Between my teaching schedule, university events, traveling, and the holidays, we always continued our fellowship over this book full of red letters. When we completed our two-year reading assignment, I graduated these students as though they'd gone through a curriculum of some sort. As a gift, all seven college students each received a downloaded MP3 version of the book of Luke to individual MP3 players and professional quality "Family of Hope" portraits—a first for them.

But it wasn't until our journey came to an end and me being back in the States, planting roots again, going back to what had been my culture, *church*, that I realized in the two years of facilitating this Bible study in China, I never taught *Christianity*.

How, how, how? How did I lead a two-year Bible study, reading the book of Luke, never teaching Christianity?

"If Christianity wasn't taught, what was?" became the resounding question.

The resounding response was, "*Love.*" Oh my gosh! For two years we'd been disciples around the *love* of God. And while we were meeting, learning about the love of God, The Family of Hope began to develop and nurture a love for each other.

This new revelation led me to one scripture. It was written of Jesus to have said, as he expounded on a new commandment that he'd given his disciples, "By this, all men will know that you are my disciples if you have love one to another."

It isn't written that one would be known as Jesus' disciples by church membership, tithing, taking communion, the Bible we carry, the crucifix we wear, the tongues we speak, the anointings we carry, by the theological degree we earned, the Christian bumper stickers adorning our cars, the clergy collars affixed to our necks, the framed ordination certificates hanging on walls, or religious rituals. Jesus didn't even say they'd be known as his disciples by the love they had for *him*. Not even by their worship of Jesus would they be known as his students.

Not by a church the disciples founded, not by a self-titled book written of their experiences as they followed their Rabbi, not even the good news revivals initiated by them, but rather that when their relationships and the fellowship with each other would be observed, someone would declare, "They must have been taught by that Jesus guy. They really do love each other."

The love of God changed my life, and it is this love that I desire to be identified by.

Are you curious?

Date: _____

ONE OF US

JANUARY 20, 2013
How did God know evil?

P.S. MAY 13, 2019
Moses wrote, "Then the LORD God said, 'Behold, the man has become like one of Us, to know good and evil. And now, lest he put out his hand and take also of the tree of life, and eat, and live forever.' "

God knowing evil is extremely intriguing, leaving me with the question of "How so? How did God know evil? Did He create it?"

Maybe this is a good time to share how often I am curious about and aware of the fact that the writer of Genesis, most popularly believed to be Moses, was not there "in the beginning." I've done, what I believe to be, due diligence in looking for how long after the entrance of Adam and Eve into the world, did Moses write the book called Genesis. It has proven difficult to find the difference in time between Adam and Eve's arrival to the world and Moses' birth, never mind the difference in time between Adam and Eve's relocation out of the Garden of Eden and the writing of the Book of Genesis.

What if Moses came into an awareness that gave birth to questions as to why life was as he experienced and observed it?

What if Moses was human and asked some of the same questions we ask? Questions like, "What is all of this about?" "Why are we here?" "Where did we come from?" or "Why can't we all just get along?"

With more access than Moses had to resources, humanity, still today, has questions.

In the writing of this verse, quotation marks are used. Moses is quoting, as it seems, what God said to Himself, about Adam and Eve's choice in eating of the Tree of Knowledge. But placing myself there, in the Garden at this juncture of the story, left me with a few questions.

Who heard God say, "They have become like one of us, knowing good and evil?" Did those same ears hear God say, "Let us make man in our image and in our likeness?"

Moses writes the statement, using quotation marks, as though he heard God say it to Himself in the moment it was said.

As the story reads, no one was there but Adam and Eve. If God was talking to Himself, would Adam and Eve have heard Him? Was God speaking to Himself audibly?

I digress but felt led to ask this January 2013 question, anew.

If our God knew evil, why?

Did God create the concept of evil? If so, why?

Why, Moses, would God create evil but punish humans for expressing it?

Are you curious?

Date: _____

HE WON'T GET YOU

APRIL 4, 2013

I had the privilege of participating in setting up an Easter egg hunt for a very special young man. His dad hid an egg by the neighbor's fence, who happened to have a dog on the other side of it. The closer Junior got to the fence to pick up the egg he found, the louder the bark got and the closer the dog came to the other side. Junior was hesitant, but his daddy said, "It's okay son, he won't get you." The dog never stopped barking right at the fence, but Junior heard his daddy say it was okay. Junior picked the egg up with no more hesitation.

So much can be said about this experience but what stands out today, is the notion of fighting with/against a defeated devil. What sense does it make to fight a fenced in dog? No, thank you. I am done binding a bound devil, cursing a cursed devil, casting out a cast in devil. God said, "It's okay, Chandrika, he won't get you."

What devil?

The enemy of what, who?

No, I am not giving any more time to acknowledging what has no power. Junior didn't go on to address the dog on the other side of the fence. He didn't say, "My Daddy said . . ." As a matter of fact, neither did his father address the noise on the other side.

Once this father spoke to his son, the son hearing his father's voice, the reality of the father became the reality of his son.

It was written of Jesus to have said, "become like little children . . ." Junior just reached out to grab what was his, what he found, what had been prepared for him.

We scream and holler at what God is giving no attention. This father has a relationship with his son and vice versa. Neither of them have a relationship with that noisy dog on the other side of the fence.

Some of us have more of (or equal to) a relationship with a defeated devil than with the God who brought us into relationship with Him.

"It's okay, Son; he won't get you."

Now I have more time and freedom to focus only on all that has been prepared for me.

P.S. JUNE 11, 2019

I lived an entire Chinese school year never addressing a devil. The most shocking part of that reality was that I didn't realize an entire year had gone by, in another country, while this devil hadn't been a part of my conversation and neither did I hear of it from any of my Western Christian teaching partners. I'd experienced one of the best years of my adult life while never binding, shutting up, breaking the back of, calling a liar, of this devil. It took returning to the States, back to church as I'd known it, to recognize I'd lived an entire year never speaking of or praying against this "adversary."

"What has happened to me, God?!" was my first question. It frightened me, this awakening. Was I going to hell because of this year long absence of a devil?

This awakening challenged me to put this experience to the test, to be intentional about living life absent of including a devil in my prayer life or daily consideration and conversation.

"Going through" became "growing through," trials became challenges, opportunities to grow, or opportunities to see God in it. I stopped being and saying, "I am under attack," or "the devil thought he had me." I resigned my participation in the celebration that comes with the congregational reminder of "satan's defeat," as I gathered with other parishioners.

What if, as preached, this devil really is defeated? Many people hear this sentiment weekly, as they gather. But, what if? What if we were still experiencing pain, disappointment, heartbreaks, inconveniences, all while this devil is defeated?

I asked myself the aforementioned questions. As a result, I was led to greater wisdoms and back to taking responsibility for my own actions. I use the wisdom gained in response to some of the challenges life presents even today.

The greatest realization of not "practicing the devil," is that it left me with the decision to be grateful in everything, no matter what the "everything" looks like. The admonishment Paul gave when writing, "In everything give thanks: for this is the will of God in Christ Jesus concerning you," became so much more tangible for me. When I am challenged with an illness, "God, I thank You for wholeness." When I am challenged with provision, "God, I thank You that I am provided for." When I am challenged in a relationship, "God, I thank You for wisdom and peace."

As the Easter treasure was prepared and set out for Junior to claim, so it is with my Father God. I will journey through and to, being consumed with gratefulness for all that has been prepared for me.

Resist the devil?

What devil?

Are you curious?

Date: _____

A UNIVERSAL CIRCLE

SEPTEMBER 18, 2013

I've just recently learned that having Type O blood means I can give blood to anyone who needs it. All is right with the world. This Chandrika, post China, just doesn't want to limit or lock herself into one group of people, and now, it all makes much more sense. The thing is, if I give blood, it is going to anyone who needs it no matter their religious beliefs (or the lack thereof), ethnicity, short comings, offenses, culture, or sexual preference. Whether faithful or unfaithful to spouses, abusive to children, abusive to women, those who steal, lie, murder, it doesn't matter. If I give blood, it could go to anyone.

Without personal agenda, am I willing to give? This is the "answered" question. There isn't any contacting me to ask my thoughts about one's lifestyle before disbursing the blood I've given. The blood is disbursed to where the need is.

I believe love is supposed to look like this.

My blood given is disbursed without limit, without boundary, without judgment, without personal agenda.

Just love people.

Loving people is not my greatest calling but the *only* calling and I am prioritizing it. I'm not being made into what it takes to love as I should, but rather being stripped of what keeps me from being the love I was created from.

Are you curious?

Date: _____

GIVEN, I AM

SEPTEMBER 19, 2013

"How can we be created in the image of a given God and not be given ourselves?"

From the very idea of ME, God was given . . . of whose image I was created in. So I am given. If I am living, I am giving. Of course, the place from which I give matters but, regardless, I am giving. Now that this reality is clear, I have to be responsible for the place in which I live so that in my constant giving, love is experienced by those who receive.

P.S. JUNE 20, 2019

given [giv-uh n] verb 1. past participle of give.

During my first year in China, I did not tithe. I gave much of my teen and adult life to the practice of tithing but didn't realize I'd not tithed for an entire year until my return to the States and to church.

I'd put into practice this method of giving for much of my life but, while abroad, became totally unaware of the ritual and how it was once a priority.

How did being in China for a year make me completely oblivious to something I'd done for so long?

In response to this question, the Lord pointed out that while I'd been in China, all of who I am had been given to Him. I was offering ten percent of my American earnings, but my life wasn't entirely yielded to the God in whose name I was giving money. Not even ten percent of my Chinese earnings seem to compare to the place of full surrender.

It seemed as though God was saying, "I'd rather have all of you than ten percent of your earnings."

But how could this sentiment of full surrender preferred over tithing be justified from Christianity's point of view and where in scripture can it be found?

Nevertheless, it isn't in the ancient biblical text that I find confirmation but rather in what I believe to be true about my "in the beginning." Just as much as I was created in the image and likeness of my parents, I believe we all were created in the image and likeness of God who is, given. Just as a mother's physical existence, at the point of conception, is given to her unborn child without inhibition, such is God.

But, it can't be that God is given and I not be the same.

At the conception of God's idea of me, He was given. While given, I believe God used Himself, His nature, as a prototype in the formation of my existence.

If God is given, I am.

Freedom!

The day I accepted the "past participle of give" as a part of my nature, calculating percentages was no longer an option, and I decided to jump off the cliff called religion to watch God carry me. This new freedom released me to managing only the place from which I give, offering out of a given state of being, ensuring that those on the receiving end of my given nature receive solely from the place of love.

Because living is giving.

Are you curious?

Date: _____

_____

_____

_____

_____

_____

_____

_____

_____

_____

_____

_____

_____

_____

_____

_____

_____

_____

_____

_____

_____

_____

_____

_____

_____

_____

_____

WHY ASK FOR MORE?

NOVEMBER 19, 2013

. . . they didn't.

It isn't recorded that the woman known as The Samaritan went back for more of Jesus.

This journal entry title, a question of thought, originates from the constant meeting of Christians week after week, year after year, asking for more of Jesus. As was written, Jesus told the Samaritan woman if she drank the water He gave, she would never thirst again. The woman exited her encounter with Jesus, leaving behind the waterpot she showed up with. She didn't need it anymore! She had a run-in with the truth, perhaps the water Jesus gives!

The Samaritan woman isn't the only person who had one life-changing encounter with Jesus. Zacchaeus had one visit with Jesus. Mark 5, the demon possessed guy begs to follow Jesus, of which Christianity implores, but Jesus tells him to go home to his friends and family. Need I go on to mention the five lepers? Or maybe the woman with the issue of blood? If it's true that it takes time to build a relationship, these folks didn't. They didn't return, repeatedly, to sit at the feet of Jesus. There was no staying to build relationship. And when one man seemed to ask for a relationship after Jesus dismissed his demons, the demon-freed fellow was admonished to go home to the people he already had relationships with.

Why weren't the people who actually met Jesus encouraged to have a "relationship with him," as Christianity has done? Why is there no record of them going to Jesus again and again asking for more of him in their lives?

P.S. JUNE 14, 2019

When do I have time to actually be who God created me to be?

I spent so much time asking God for more of Him, for more of Him in my life, there was no time to be His image. I came to believe that as long as we keep asking God for more, it absolves us from actualizing the being of His created likeness. The continual asking for more of Jesus, is reflective of a focus on who or what we are not, making it difficult to be who and what we are.

God has done what He is "going to do" so, I don't need more.

I need to do my best at being who He created me to be. This is the "more" I need.

Are you curious?

Date: _____

SIDE EYE

I opened my Bible to Genesis to read about the exit of Adam and Eve from the Garden. The first place my eye lands on, Genesis 3:14: "So the Lord God said to the serpent: 'Because you have done this, you are cursed more than all cattle, and more than every beast of the field; On your belly you shall go, and you shall eat dust all the days of your life.' "

Slow down.

Does that read, "You are cursed more than all cattle and more than every beast of the field?"

Immediately my imagination traveled back to when the cattle and beast were created. Genesis 1:25, "God made the wild animals according to their kinds, the livestock according to their kinds, and all the creatures that move along the ground according to their kinds. And God saw that it was good."

Cattle was seen as good in Genesis chapter one, but when reading God cursed the serpent *more than* the beast and cattle, the more than implies the beast and cattle were *previously* or even *created* cursed. Huh?

The word cursed in its original meaning is the Hebrew word "execrate" and is defined "declare to be evil or detestable, to denounce, or to detest utterly."

According to what Moses wrote, God declared the serpent more evil and more detestable than the beast and cattle.

Is it just me or am I reading that Moses believes God thought the cattle and beast of the field, that He created, as evil and utterly detestable? This, after reading that God looked at all He created and said, "It is good"?

P.S. JULY 9, 2019
insert side eye

Are you curious?

Date: _____

CALLED TO MY OWN

JULY 13, 2015
The show *First 48* presents evidence of a crime, or evidence of an experience. While viewing the presentation, the audience may observe a lifeless body, bloody surfaces, a clue of the weapon used, etc. The aforementioned evidence is *not* the experience but *proof* of an experience.

Simply put, God has not called us to the evidence pointing to Him. He has called us to the experience with our name on it.

Paul the apostle left evidence of his experience, thirteen letters. Moses left evidence of his experience, five books. David left evidence of his experience, seventy plus songs. John left evidence of his experience, one book and I am leaving mine.

We have focused so much on studying the evidence left, we are missing out on the experience designated for us, the one designated for us by a God who is bigger than the evidence.

P.S. OCTOBER 1, 2019
After spending two months reading scripture upon scripture upon scripture, I read the last verse of the book of Revelation, closed the book, and the voice God said one thing:

"Now that you have studied everyone else's experience of me, I am ready to give you your own."

Evidenced by the Biblical Studies Bachelor of Arts Degree displayed on a shelf in my home, I committed to four years of higher education attempting to study what so many others of the past believed of their personal experiences of God. But with just two or so months of reading each volume of this book, the Bible, I learned there is and has always been, a personal experience of God designated for me.

Are you curious?

Date: _____

OFFENDED? WHO?

JANUARY 28, 2016

Christianity teaches that Adam and Eve committed the *original* or, first sin.

The word "sin," in its simplest form, is defined as *offender*.

Sin, when it is first mentioned in the Bible, doesn't mean "to offend God."

To be perceived as an offender, there must be one negatively impacted by the egregious behavior of another. The person or persons negatively impacted by the egregious behavior of another, becomes the offended. Offended is defined as "resentful or annoyed, typically as a result of a perceived insult."

The word "offender" is only validated by an experience that has left someone insulted.

As Moses writes, he doesn't offer that God was offended by Adam and Eve's decision to disregard the commandment given not to eat of the tree.

The first mention of sin, according to Moses, can be found as a part of Cain and Abel's life story in Genesis Chapter 4. This is well after their parents' impactful choice and the consequences thereof.

In the case of Adam and Eve, I ask, was God offended by their choice to eat of the tree despite the instruction not to?

Was God resentful, annoyed, and perhaps insulted by their behavior?

What if He was none of the above?

What if God was not offended by their choosing?

Are you curious?

Date: _____

PERSPECTIVE OF THE ABSENT

JANUARY 28, 2016

Evident in most Bibles, those who were born long after the experiences we read of, divided the books and letters into chapters. The titles of these divisions seem to offer a perspective of the experiences written of.

"The Fall of Man," Genesis 3.

I have many Greek and Hebrew resources to learn more about the original languages of the scriptures. But what source, other than the dictionary, can I use for the chapter titles in the Bible? These titles originate from the perspectives of those who weren't there for the experiences we are reading about.

In using the dictionary to define "Fall" I found twenty-nine different definitions. It is my thought that the first three definitions listed, giving meaning to the word, are prevalently used.

Fall: *1. To drop or descend under the force of gravity, as to a lower place through loss or lack of support. 2. To come or drop down suddenly to a lower position, especially to leave a standing or erect position suddenly, whether voluntarily or not. 3. To become less or lower; become of a lower level, degree, amount, quality, value, number, etc.*

Being raised a Christian, the third definition stands out to me the most. I can't find this definition in the narrative of Adam and Eve. I don't read where God told Adam and Eve they fell, that they'd become less or lower than a man and woman created in the image and likeness of God. Where is it written that this couple lost a degree of the dominion and blessing in the fingerprint of their divine molecularity? I don't read where who they were decreased in quality or value.

Because this chapter title, like so many others in the Bible, was given by one who was absent of the experience, looking it up in the "original language" of the Old Testament isn't an option. "So, after man fell . . ." is something I've been repeating for as long as I can remember but if I am going to preach it, what is meant by it should be important, I believe.

As it relates to Adam and Eve's garden experience, I, being absent, adopted and preached the perspective of the absent. The author wasn't there, being born on the "after" side of creation. Moses was absent at The Beginning but writes its story. Was it his writing, regardless of his absence, that opened the door to others who would, in the future, offer their perspective despite their absence?

Did Adam *fall*? Did Eve *fall*?

If they fell, to what place did they descend?

More importantly, did God see them as fallen?

Are you curious?

Date: _____

DID THEY STUDY THE MAIL?

SEPTEMBER 30, 2016

"Study to show yourself approved unto God, a workman need not be ashamed, rightly dividing the word of truth."

If the Bible didn't exist when Paul wrote to Timothy, what was he referring to as the "word of truth" in the letter containing that instruction?

P.S. OCTOBER 10, 2019

There is nothing in the Bible that says study the Bible.

Who told us to?

The word study in the letter of Paul to Timothy is not defined as "research or a detailed examination and analysis of a subject, phenomenon."

Four years of Biblical education, ordination class, and over $100,000 in student loans later, I realized God never intended for me to study scripture.

Did Timothy study the letter Paul mailed to him?

Did the Corinthian congregants have a Bible study over the mailed letter titled First and Second?

The early church couldn't have studied what has been dubbed as the Synoptic Gospels, those books weren't published yet. Paul's letters were archived but was it done so that future generations could study them for decades, upon decades, upon decades?

Nevertheless, Christianity has created an entire system, an expensive system, around studying mailed letters to the assembly at Rome, Galatia, Philippi, Ephesus, etc.

Lord, were we called to study the mail, so as to copy and compare our personal experience or revelation of You to what was written in them?

Are you curious?

Date: _____

NARRATIVE OWNERSHIP

FEBRUARY 16, 2015
"Adam and Eve did not write their own story."

P.S. NOVEMBER 7, 2019
I once read: Always ask yourself, "Who writes the story?" "Who benefits from the story?" "Who is missing from the story?"

The authorship of Genesis is attributed to a man who was not there "In the Beginning."

While reading the first three and a half chapters of Genesis, I noticed there was a person missing from the story being told, the author. Moses, the writer, born well after creation, wrote about it.

Being aware of Moses's absence from the event of creation gave me pause, pause pregnant with curiosity.

Here are a few questions of interest . . .

Did Adam know he had been created in the image and likeness of God and what it all meant?

Did Eve know her origin was that from a man's rib?

Did Adam relay to Eve the instruction he received about not eating of the Tree of Knowledge of Good and Evil?

Before the conversation with a serpent, had Eve been informed of the dominion over the earth given to her?

We are living in a time when owning or controlling our narrative is all the buzz.

What if one of today's personal narrative buzz phrases existed when Adam and Eve were living? How would they have told or written their own story? How would their children have written the story of their family dynamic? What would this first family write if they owned their narrative? If this family lived in the day of social media, what hashtags would they assign to their perceived personal story?

It would seem important to be aware that Adam and Eve, Cain and Able, had a perspective of their life experience and it should matter to those of us who champion the Bible as it's religious authority.

Lord, how different would this whole thing called religion be if the narrative Moses wrote had been written by those who were actually there in the beginning?

Are you curious?

Date: _____

UNLISTED

MAY 21, 2016

If hell is real, a place where unbelieving and misbehaving souls go after death to burn for an eternity, why isn't it listed among the places created in the beginning?

Are you curious?

Date: _____

UNDESERVING, UNWORTHY

SEPTEMBER 23, 2017

As one who held the title of worship leader, leading with songs to and about God while the lyrics celebrated the concept of our unworthiness and *undeservingness* causes personal dissonance for me. Those kinds of lyrics are, in large part, desired. Songs of brokenness, of desperation, seem to yield the response that participants feel as necessary for their worship experience.

But does God see or has He ever seen His creation as undeserving and unworthy?

When I was in high school, a few of my teachers would begin the semester by giving an A to every student in our class. We had to prove we believed about ourselves what he or she did; that we were deserving of the A already given.

Grace, as defined by Christianity, is God's unmerited or undeserved kindness to us. But what if we all actually started the semester of our life's existence with an A? Why? Because we were deserving of it. To deserve is to show qualities worthy of. Because I believe God created us in His image and in His likeness, I believe He sees in us qualities that are worthy of.

While Christianity proclaims God's worthiness and deservingness, the religion proclaims its unworthiness and *undeservingness*. If God is deserving, why aren't we—His reflection—deserving? If God is worthy, why aren't we—His reflection—worthy?

I believe it is extremely important that we see ourselves as God sees us. In my own personal relationship, I'd adopted this whole notion of grace. But the more I begin to see myself as the image of God in which I'd been created, the concept of grace began to make less sense. The more I became aware of myself as

171

God's reflection, seeing myself as undeserving of His kindness decreased. Seeing myself as God sees me gave me pause, as if He'd ever seen me as undeserving of His kindness.

In my experience of being a daughter, I can't imagine my parents changing their minds about who they believe me to be, changing their minds about how deserving they believe me to be because of disagreeable behavior. Many times, I didn't follow their instructions, I didn't obey, but they never changed their minds about who I am, what I deserve, and how worthy I am.

What would life or the world be like for many of us, even those read of in the Bible, if we believed we came into this world "with an A?" What if we believed God never changed His mind about us no matter what, that He will never see us as undeserving or unworthy of His kindness?

Let's imagine a world where this notion of grace, the undeserved kindness of God, doesn't exist. Imagine a world where we don't see ourselves as undeserving, as unworthy of kindness from the one who created us but, instead, reflecting the reason we are deserving and worthy of this kindness that is God.

P.S. NOVEMBER 15, 2019
Must we see ourselves as underserving and unworthy in the sight of God to be worshippers of His presence?

Are you curious?

Date: _____

HE SAID, SHE SAID

OCTOBER 15, 2016
The Bible does not speak, it is not vocal.

P.S. OCTOBER 25, 2019
Despite what is customarily declared by many of us, the Bible does not speak.

I sat down to read this book, to read the books in the book, but as I began, my reading shifted. I transitioned from reading the book to reading of and about people. It became common practice to read human experiences of God and interpretations thereof rather than reading what "the Bible says."

People said. Therefore, those people wrote. Much of the scriptures read of *people hearing, saying, and documenting.* Humans heard God speak, *said* what they *heard,* and what they *said* was *written.*

Questions birthed from the abandonment of "the Bible says" released me to a freedom in my relationship with God I'd never known.

One reality this fortieth decade of life has taught me; I don't have to invest myself in the stories of everyone I meet. It isn't mandatory to invest in the stories of all my friends and family. With intention, I choose what stories and the people sharing them to invest in.

Christianity preaches that the characters in which its textual authority reads, are real people, people with stories. For me, the same applies in being intentional about which of those people and the stories attached to them is worth my investment.

Throwing away "The Bible says . . ." widened my perspective as I read these ancient pages.

Proverbs 31. Coming up as a young lady, desiring to be married, the ambition was to be the woman described in this chapter. Growing up, and still today, I only heard, what I now know as, Proverbs 31:10 through to the last verse of that chapter. Even as I studied in Bible college, the only part of the chapter that stood out to me was "Who can find a virtuous woman? For her price is far above rubies." This question and response was popularly quoted in my pubescent hearing. Then one day in conversation, post-The-Bible-says dismissal, a gentleman mentioned this "Proverbs 31 Woman" in our exchange about marriage. His passionately expressed point of view encouraged me to revisit the text again because something about his unrealistic expectations, set according to this particular proverb, rubbed me the wrong way.

"The sayings of King Lemuel—an inspired utterance his mother taught him."

Wait.

What?

Proverbs 31 opens offering this chapter as an utterance, a desire this mother taught her son.

Now, after relinquishing "The Bible says . . ." I have questions.

Who is Lemuel's mother?

How'd she grow up?

From where did her desire originate?

Was this utterance handed down to her from generations past?

Was she the woman she desired for her son?

Did my mother have the same desire for her daughters?

Here I was, because of "The Bible says . . ." endeavoring to be this "Proverbs 31 Woman." Christianity says I should be as a disciple of Jesus. But this mother taught her son the desire she had for him, most likely. This mother wanted the woman her son would marry to have the characteristics listed in this proverb.

When Lemuel's mother taught her son what she believed a virtuous woman to be, did she think it would become a proverb? Did she know that it would become "the word of God," and that women for decades to come would desire to be that woman to the sons of other mothers?

In my opinion, declaring "The Bible says . . ." dismisses the personage from those we read of while, at the same time, Christianity preaches to believe in the message of the characters. The disowning of the phrase puts breath into the bodies of these authors, families, communities, and the societies of which they were a part; freeing me to breathe, freeing me to inhale and exhale my own relationship with God.

The Bible doesn't say anything but rather, "He said, she said."

He said, "God said."

She said, "The Lord said."

They said, "Jesus said."

Lord, it is in this reality I find freedom to hear what You have to say to this *she*–to this *me*.

Are you curious?

Date: _____

MY DAYDREAM'S QUESTION

DECEMBER 2, 2016

What if Jesus never returns and the world never ends?

P.S. JUNE 12, 2020

"We're living in the last days," is what people in church were saying generations ago and many, upon examination of the world's climate, continue to declare the same.

That phrase, verbatim, was being declared before I was born, being born forty-six years ago. In my adolescence, I gave much thought to "the last days." The phrase may have been declared when my grandmother was a child and perhaps when her mother was child.

As children, we knew what was meant by it or so we thought. But now, as an adult, having heard it countlessly, I thought to look at some definitions to discontinue my childhood assumption and figure out which generation is telling the truth, finding very little confirmation.

Are these the last days? Or, were *those* the last, the days of our grands and great-grands, as they were saying so?

How long do the last days last?

Are you curious?

Date: _____

IN JESUS' NAME

APRIL 4, 2017

He said pray *in* "his name" not pray *saying* "in Jesus' name."

P.S. NOVEMBER 13, 2019

I am a triathlete and in becoming this type of athlete, opportunities to consult and train others are frequent. Teaching future triathletes to swim, coaching them on efficient open-water swimming, cycling with them, teaching the best ways to power forward in speed, and offering my experience as a runner, are just some of what I offer as a TRI consultant. In preparation to become a triathlete one has to consider equipment: bike, cleats, helmets, gloves, running shoes, swim caps, goggles, swimwear, nutrition, etc.

One of my responsibilities as a triathlete consultant is to recommend the best place to purchase these necessities to be successful. Often, I suggest where to buy a product and offer to the client, "Tell them I sent you." My heart is that the client will be treated as though they are me making the purchase. I want the client to purchase with my investment history behind them. The client is being sent in my name, using my influence, and receiving the benefits thereof.

But the aforementioned will only last as long as it takes for the client to build their own investment history, their own influence. While my client is going and purchasing in my name (investment history and influence), he or she is building their own.

When we refer to others as powerful, we are referring to their level of influence. Isn't it the same when proclaimed, "there is power in the name of Jesus?" When Jesus said, "Pray in my name," could he have been offering the use of his investment history? Was Jesus offering the benefit of his level of influence with God?

Get where I am going with this?

If I keep going to God with the history of Jesus behind me, at some point, I will begin to build an awareness of my own history, my influence.

"God, if I was created in your image and in your likeness, why am I not enough?" is the question born of my curiosity around why we say, ". . . in Jesus' name."

This is not a suggestion to end prayers saying, "In my name, amen."

Jesus' exhortation to pray in his name doesn't seem to emphasize a name as much as it may be an emphasis on position of influence.

Christ has introduced me to who I have always been, to my spiritual position, and to the history with God that began with His thought of me.

I will approach prayer in the image and likeness of God that I am and for this, "I am grateful, amen."

Are you curious?

Date: _____

"IT'S A SIN!" THEY SAID.

MAY 13, 2018

For so many years of my life, I believed engaging in sexual intercourse, before becoming a wife, to be a sin and that sin would send me to hell. The concept of *fornication* was introduced in the Old Testament and in its introduction, it was defined as the sin of adultery and idolatry. The New Testament Greek word fornication only means *sexual immorality*. Who, in Christianity, decided sexual intercourse between two, single, age-appropriate, consenting people was immoral?

I am not suggesting that such a decision is moral but for all of the fire and brimstone preaching I heard relating to the subject, surely there shouldn't be any room for question where the reality of sex is concerned.

As a kid, being taught not to engage in premarital sex because it's a sin definitely kept me fearful of what God may do to me had I indulged. But then I matured, started reading the Bible for myself, and in doing so, found that what Paul the Apostle called sin was sexual immorality, not specifically sexual intercourse between two, single, age-appropriate, consenting people.

This journal entry is not to advocate for premarital sex but to advocate for what is true. In some cases, being taught sex before marriage was against God's rules, only peeked a lot of church kids' sense of curiosity, a curiosity many satisfied at an early age. Surely truth is impactful enough in sharing one's experience of the sequence of events following the decision not to remain abstinent until marriage has the ability to influence the decisions of future generations regarding unmarried lovemaking.

My hermeneutics of premarital sex: Every choice we make has a consequence and not all consequences are bad. The decision to be abstinent until marriage comes with a cost and the decision to do the opposite comes with a cost. It is a personal decision in deciding which price one is willing to pay.

After arriving to the aforementioned conclusion, I have no regrets and it is in God's love for me that my resolve finds rest.

Are you curious?

Date: _____

THE INTERPRETATION OF INSPIRATION

JUNE 27, 2018
We have made an authority of someone else's experience of inspiration.

P.S. NOVEMBER 1, 2019
theópneustos [theh-op'-nyoo-stos] Divinely breathed in.

Inspiration is, quite literally, an experience of the physical body. It is solely personal.

Inspiration is just as much a personal experience as breathing is, i.e., its definition.

If inspiration is an experience of the human anatomy, for each human, the experience is different.

Our experience of inspiration is only evidenced by the personal interpretation of said experience. In other words, the experience of inspiration has to be interpreted by the physical body experiencing it. The evidence of interpretation is found in what inspiration produces.

"All scripture is *inspired* by God, and is profitable for doctrine, for reproof, for correction, for instruction in righteousness."[3]

There is a process in producing fruit of the experience of inspiration and that process is personal.

Lord, are we missing the "divinely breathed in" experience individually designated for us while studying the fruit of inspiration experienced by others?

---

3 I have chosen to emphasize in italics the word from this passage which I find to be exceptionally important.

Are you curious?

Date: _____

QUESTIONS OF A CRIME

AUGUST 1, 2018

As the story goes, the first homicide of the Bible was committed by the first son of Adam and Eve.

Cain, the eldest son, had the assignment of cultivating the ground while Able, the youngest son, had the responsibility of keeping the sheep.

Time came for both brothers to present an offering to the Lord, Moses writes. Cain offers fruit of the ground and Able offered the first born of the sheep. There are several questions showing up between the level of respect God had for each offering, Cain getting angry, God's warning to Cain, and Cain killing his brother.

When was giving an offering to the Lord introduced to this family?

Did Cain know what would make him and his offering respected by God?

Why did Cain believe God had no respect for his offering?

If, in this investigation, I could interview Moses, I'd ask, "Are you telling me an all-seeing God set in motion a murder?" I'd ask Moses, "Why do you believe our all-knowing God would tell Cain of his lack of respect for Him and his offering if He, the Lord God, knew it would make Cain angry enough to kill his brother?"

For me, this criminal case is still unsolved.

Are you curious?

Date: _____

THE BEST KEPT SECRET

(DISCOVERED, 2018)

Moses writes (in his book entitled Deuteronomy),

"*Be sure* to *set aside a tenth* of all that your fields *produce* each year. *Eat the tithe* of your grain, new wine and olive oil, and the firstborn of your herds and flocks in the presence of the Lord your God at the place he will choose as a dwelling for his Name, so that you may learn to revere the Lord your God always. But if that place is too distant and you have been blessed by the Lord your God and cannot carry your tithe (because the place where the Lord will choose to put his Name is so far away), then *exchange your tithe for silver*, and *take the silver with you* and go to the place the Lord your God will choose. *Use the silver to buy whatever you like:* cattle, sheep, wine or other fermented drink, or *anything you wish.* Then you and your household shall eat there in the presence of the Lord your God and rejoice. And do not neglect the Levites living in your towns, for they have no allotment or inheritance of their own. At the *end* of every *three years,* bring all the *tithe*s of *that* year's produce and store it in your towns, so that the *Levites* (who have no allotment or inheritance of their own) and the *foreigners*, the *fatherless* and the *widows* who live in your towns may come and eat and be satisfied, and so that the *Lord your God* may *bless you in all the work of your hands.*"[4]

Read it again.

Read it again.

---

4 I have chosen to emphasize in italics the words and phrases from this passage which I find to be exceptionally important.

Read it again.

Read it again.

When reading the entire book of Deuteronomy, it was through the lens of Christian indoctrination that I read Moses's instructions concerning the tithe. I missed how plainly stated these verses are.

If you are like me,

Read it again.

Read it again.

Read it again.

P.S.

From where did the instruction *"Pay* your tithes . . ." originate? In the book of Malachi, Ezra wrote, quoting God, *"Bring* the whole tithe . . ." Pay, defined, is to give (someone) money that is due for work done, goods received, or a debt incurred. Bring, the actual word used in the admonishment, is the Hebrew word meaning "to go or come." Of course, God is not calculating what it cost for His "goods received" or the "work He's done." But surely there is a psychological impact from hearing the persistent reminder to "Pay your tithes," or no?

Are you curious?

Date: _____

FRIEND REQUEST

OCTOBER 1, 2018

Western Christianity has done well to own the disciple's graduation from servants of Jesus to being friends of Jesus. Yes, at a point in their journey with Jesus, it is written of him to have said to his disciples, "I no longer call you servants, I call you friends."

Did Jesus expect, from his friends, worship?

Reflecting on that question based on personal experience, I can hardly take a compliment from a friend, never mind *worship*, and especially the brand of worship many Christians, including myself, offer to Jesus. There is probably not a "Friend of Jesus" song I've not sung in my time of personal devotion or led as a worship leader.

But what kind of friend willingly accepts or even expects worship?

What kind of friend wants public recognition, religiously, for manifested goodness in the lives of all mankind?

What kind of friend wants a bowed knee and a prostrate body at its feet?

John, a disciple, writes of this initiation, of sorts. Jesus is noted to have offered the reason for such transition in his relationship with these particular followers. The shift in Jesus' perspective of how he associated with the twelve, was based on giving to them all he knew of his Father.

As a result of shared knowledge and the divvying of information, a common collective was formed. The impartation of information empowered them and empowerment is an equalizer. Friends.

But where, in the place of equality, can worship be found?

197

One should never lose respect when one is equal to another but note there is a difference between respect and worship.

Personally, the initial question is so impactful, there is no prolific way to end this entry, except, to ask one last question: If Jesus did not expect the worship of his friends, what did he expect?

Are you curious?

Date: _____

SELAH

OCTOBER 15, 2018

My Prayer: "Lord, I want to be closer to You."

God's Response: "There has never been distance between you and me. The distance has been between your religious perspective and the reality of being made in my image and likeness."

Are you curious?

Date: _____

LOVE CONFRONTS

OCTOBER 12, 2019

A few authors of whose books we read in the Bible proclaim the unchanging nature of God. To add, John writes of God's love for the world, and I continuously experience God as love.

So it is, our God's love does not change.

God has and will always exist as love.

For me, it is the aforementioned belief that confronts what Moses writes as the sequence of events following Adam and Eve eating of the Tree of the Knowledge of Good and Evil. The great multiplying of sorrow, pain in conception, longing for the husband, the rulership of a husband she'd long for, cursing the ground to produce thorns and thistles, Adam toiling said ground, eating salty and soggy bread because of his new sweaty occupation; all until the day of death. Never mind the expired access to the place in which they were created, the Garden of Eden.

Christianity would like me to believe the above-mentioned as a part of God's response to Adam and Eve's choice to eat of the Tree. But the love of God I have experienced doesn't add to the natural sequence of events following a bad judgment call. Rather, God loves us through the consequence.

My life was and continues to be transformed by this love that is God and that same love confronts what Moses writes as a part of the sequence of events. Why wasn't it enough of a consequence that their eyes, Adam and Eve's, were opened to a reality not promised to them?

Why wasn't knowing good and evil enough of a consequence?

Why would God, who loves me unconditionally, add more?

P.S. SEPTEMBER 9, 2020

In third person, Moses writes that God looked at all He had made, including male and female, seeing the very good of what He created. However, Adam and Eve, according to the story, were both prohibited from knowing *good*.

Why would whom God created as good be forbidden from an *awareness* of good?

On this wise, the disallowance of knowing *good* would have been, for this couple, a disallowance of *self-awareness*. Knowing *good* would have been to know themselves as they had been made. Therefore, according to this narrative, as I see it, being identified by God as good was permissible but for these two humans having a personal awareness of themselves good, was not.

It would seem difficult to teach such a narrative as theology in this era of positive thinking, self-love, self-awareness, self-affirmation, personal empowerment, etc. Speaking for myself, I have been connected to people who benefited more from me when I did not *know* the good I am.

Must I believe God intended the same for His creation? Must I believe God needed me to be ignorant to the good He created me as that He might benefit more, from my being? Must I believe God to be insecure in His Godness? Must I believe God needs my existence to be His God-self?

I have too many questions to continue being fully invested in the aforementioned detail of how we and the world as we've known it, came to be. Reclaiming my time!

Are you curious?

Date: _____

JOVONDA'S QUESTION OF MANIFESTATION

OCTOBER 14, 2019

"How do I take charge of my thoughts to consistently manifest the great things God has for me?"

My Offering: I can't tell you how to take charge of your thoughts to see God's manifestation of the great things He has for you. However, manifestation became my life experience after accepting who and how I believe God created me. I discontinued seeing myself apart from God, who lacks nothing, who is literally unacquainted with the idea of insufficiency. When I stopped believing I was broken, that my soul needed to be fixed, I began to consistently experience God's manifestation. When I stopped chasing or desiring to be like Him but accepted that I had never existed outside of the image and likeness of God, manifestation became my reality. Manifesting as God sees me yields the manifestation of all things good, all things God, and I do my best to avoid participating in anything contradictory to that place of existence.

Are you curious?

Date: _____

A NEED, A TREE, A CHOICE

OCTOBER 30, 2019

Christianity teaches that a lamb was slain and that lamb was Jesus; the lamb being symbolic of the character of Christ and his body sacrificed.

The lamb was slain from the foundation of the world, John the Elder writes in the Book of Revelation.

Christianity teaches that God came from Heaven in the form of Jesus, the Lamb slain, to be the ransom for what would be a sinful humanity.

=

God, before the world was conceived, decided to come to Earth as a man, to redeem the humans He created, because those created humans would eat from a forbidden tree created by Him, God.

Pause

God created man, set in place the possibility for failure, so that He could, in the future, manifest as a savior? A hero?

Proceed

To believe Jesus was slain before the world's conception, would be to believe God had the idea to create a world He would have to save. I'd have to believe God had a need and out of it He created a crisis that would form in us a longing to be saved from said crisis. For as it is, a hero is only necessary in times of need.

Did God have a need, one so great, that He planned to come to the world as its savior before creating it?

If the scripture read that Adam and Eve complied with the admonishment not to eat of the Tree of the Knowledge of Good and Evil, God's predestined plan to come to the world as the lamb slain, according to John's revelation, would have been thwarted.

How then would God have been glorified by mankind except He be a savior? How then could God be a savior, except there be a need? How then could there be a need, except there be a tree and a choice? And how could there be a tree and a choice except God created it?

"John, are you saying all of this was planned?"

Are you curious?

Date: _____

WHAT IS, "IF IT'S NOT IN THE BIBLE, IT'S NOT GOD?" FOR ALL I HAVE, ALEX.

NOVEMBER 1, 2019

Language gifted, letters gathered, words drafted, pages bonded, all in the realm of time, about an often indefinable, uncontainable, timeless, immeasurable, indestructible reality; the Spirit that is God.

Are you curious?

Date: _____

iREPENT

NOVEMBER 21, 2019

I believe what Jeremiah wrote as a part of his experience of God, "Before you were formed in the womb, I knew you." There is more to that verse, as Jeremiah heard, but these first ten words stand out to me.

It led me to ask God, "Who is the me You knew before I was formed in the womb of my mother?"

During my two-year residency in China, learning who I was not, became a class I attended on a regular basis. I left the States as a licensed minister, degreed in Biblical Studies, with plenty of church leadership experience. But none of the aforementioned mattered as a resident in a country who spied on my daily activity, assuming I was there to initiate and facilitate an underground church.

This was an opportune time to self-reflect on all I had become but could not be in another part of the world:

Who am I now?

Who am I without the use of a microphone, a church stage, my church title(s), my religious education?

Living in a country where my religion is practically illegal, who was I without everything identifying me as a Christian?

Who was I without the crucifix around my neck?

Who was I without the Bible I carried everywhere daily?

It was written of Jesus to have stated, as he spoke to a stranger, "God is a Spirit." Believing God to be none of my ministry accomplishments, a religious classification, the symbolism adorning my collar nor the two Testaments I carried, I began a process of stripping away everything veiling God's perspective of my existence. I am always grateful to the Lord for His idea of me and this stripping away of Christianity is the process of exchanging my idea of me for His.

Therein lies the reason for this particular position of repentance at this point in my relationship with God. And by repentance, I mean, to think differently. Before thinking, then thinking differently, Christianity limited my experience of God.

I will never cease in exchanging my perspective of self for the me that God knew.

Yes Lord, I repent.

Are you curious?

Date: _____

THE MISTAKE GOD MADE

NOVEMBER 26, 2019

David's Prayer (Psalms 51:10): Create in me a clean heart, oh God, and renew in me a right spirit.

My Prayer: Create in me a clean heart and renew in me a right spirit.

God's response to my prayer: Are you suggesting I didn't do it right the first time? Are you saying I fell short of creating you in my image and in my likeness?

Me: But, it's in the Bible, Lord. This prayer is an Old Testament scripture, remember?

God: I created you, with a pure heart. Are you asking Me, in whom failure cannot be found, to create, again, your spiritual posture? Your prayer implies I made a mistake and need to go back and start over. But if I am God, perfect in all of my ways, "Lord make me over" is not a statement you should entertain.

Me: Yes Lord, I hear. Yes Lord, I will continue to practice seeing myself as You see me. Thank You, Lord, for Your idea of me and for creating complete, who I am.

Are you curious?

Date: _____

PROTEST

NOVEMBER 29, 2019
All Quotation Marks Matter!
With much appreciation,
The Bible

P.S.
If only the Bible could actually speak.

Are you curious?

Date: _____

KNOCKING AT THE DOOR OF A SUNDAY SCHOOL LESSON

DECEMBER 1, 2019

Genesis 6 reads that God was sad about creating humans, seeing how great man's wickedness had become and all inclinations of every heart being only evil. Moses writes of God's solution, to wipe mankind (animals, birds, and creatures), whom He created, from the face of the earth.

This Genesis narrative precedes the story of Noah building the Ark. In large part, it is Noah, God's favor of him, his family, animals, and the boat he built that we heard stories of as children. The Sunday School lesson began with, "But Noah found grace in the eyes of the Lord . . ." However, I don't recall hearing of the circumstances surrounding the need for his favor.

To teach children that wickedness, evil, and corruption continued to exist after God caused the flood, as the story is written, could be a bit of a challenge, I suppose. But now, as an educated adult reader, I have questions aside from the juvenile version of Noah's story and his call to construction work.

If I could go back to Sunday School and inquire of the teacher about this lesson, I'd ask, "Did God, who knows everything, know His solution would not change what made Him sad?" I'd ask, "Does the fact that wickedness still remains mean all of the Earth's inhabitants who perished in the flood were drowned for no reason?" then follow up with, "Were the men, women, and children of that time unredeemable? Why wouldn't their wickedness, evil, and corruption be covered by the foreordained plan for Jesus to die for the sins of the whole world, as is taught? After it was all done, everyone dead, did God feel bad about what

He'd done?" and "What is the difference between God causing a mass drowning and a man committing a mass shooting?"

While revisiting this not-so-simple story, "God saw . . ." got my attention.

In choosing to believe we were created in the image and likeness of God, believing nothing has ever changed that reality, God has never seen our existence apart from His. For God to "see" in the direction of His creation but not see Himself, would be to completely disconnect, disassociate, and detach Himself from, Himself. The Lord would have to see His creation apart from Himself to eradicate it.

I curl up into the fetal position and weep at the announcement of another mass shooting because I see myself in those whose lives were ended. It is also heartbreaking to imagine the circumstances that would lead to such a disconnect, disassociation, and detachment of a person who'd commit such an atrocity. Groups of men, women, and children living as a part of our world, wiped out by someone who had the ability to pull a trigger.

But . . .

Isn't this what God did, according to the story surrounding Noah and his family? God, having the ability to do so, used what He created, pulled the trigger, to wipe out all whom He created; thousands, millions, billions of people.

Being a part of group prayers for mass-shooting victims, even the offender, all while preaching a God who committed mass murder is no longer an option for me. To preach this story of Noah and the grace he was afforded is to be at peace with many lives lost, including the children born as a result of man's corruption, as is written.

Not the God I love.

No, thank you.

Are you curious?

Date: _____

MY PATERNAL ANNOUNCEMENT

DECEMBER 15, 2019

If only I could remember the actual day of showing up to have a conversation with God, but upon arrival, the usual offering of preliminaries was unnecessary. It was years into our relationship, but this time was different from any other time before. I was already sitting at the table. It felt like I'd been there, having never left. It felt like home. I was where I'd always been, tuning in to a conversation that had never ended, and I loved it.

But how could I, as Paul writes and Christianity preaches, be "adopted by God," "adopted into the family of God?" How then could I embrace the theology of the "Spirit of adoption" when God never stopped seeing me as His child?

I find it difficult to imagine what it's like to be adopted, as we were reared by our biological parents, my sisters and me. It would seem easy to celebrate the thought of being adopted by God if I were acquainted with being disconnected from my provenance and chosen to join another family as a part of my life experience. Not even Paul the apostle, who introduced this adoption theology, knows the experience of being adopted. How was he able to celebrate such a concept as a part of his life's testimony, never knowing what it was like to be disconnected from his bloodline while qualifying for the inheritance of a bloodline not belonging to him?

To embrace this idea of the family of God taking me in as its own, I'd have to believe I came to exist by other means. I'd have to believe my spiritual existence was fashioned by another, another who is not God. But because God has only seen me as His own, I feel limitless, boundless. It is the reason religion is extremely claustrophobic, this eternal perspective God has of me. I find more abundance in human fellowship than church membership simply because, God has never disassociated Himself from the very essence of who I am, of who we are.

How Paul came to believe adoption as his portion isn't clear to me, but hope can be found in his declaration of an inheritance for the "spiritually adopted." However, our identity is reflected in the lineage of our eternal existence, making the hope of inheritance unnecessary while accepting all of whom we are as enough.

My priority is the identity of the image that is the likeness of God, who has always been and will forever be my Beginning.

Are you curious?

Date: _____

... AS WAS SUPPOSED?

MARCH 9, 2020

My original question relating to Matthew's genealogy of Jesus was "If Jesus was not born of Joseph's seed, being born of a virgin, why is he declared a descendant of David if Joseph is not his biological father?"

But then there is Luke's genealogy of Jesus.

At the opening of Luke's book, he offers the reason for which he writes his letter. Luke, who was not one of Jesus' twelve disciples, writes the results of what he called a "careful investigation" of beliefs handed down from the first eyewitnesses and servants of the word. It is Luke's desire to investigate all that he had learned inspiring my fearlessness in asking questions of the teachings handed down to me of the Christian tradition.

Luke's genealogy of Jesus is prefaced with how Jesus' ministry began. The wilderness cry of John the Baptist, his introduction of one coming who was mightier that he, and his imprisonment for such a declaration, Jesus' baptisms and descending of the Holy Ghost upon him, and God's pleasure expressed for His son, are some of the details of what was a bombshell discovery for me!

"And Jesus himself began his ministry at about thirty years of age, *being (as was supposed) the son of Joseph*, the son of Heli."[5]

New questions alert!

"He was the son, *so it was thought*, of Joseph," the New International Version reads.

It was *thought*?

---

5 I have chosen to emphasize in italics the words and phrases from this passage which I find to be exceptionally important.

Christianity taught me Jesus was born of a virgin, but could it be the eyewitnesses and servants of the word, those Luke interviewed, didn't believe Mary, the mother of Jesus, to be a virgin? Did these eyewitnesses believe Joseph to be the biological father of Jesus?

For so many years I heard, "Jesus! Born of a virgin, died, and rose again! He is the son of David and the seed of Abraham!" and "Jesus! Born of a virgin, down through thirty and two generations!" But how can Jesus be born of a virgin woman while, at the same time, be connected through the patriarchal lineage of Abraham and David?

Having such questions and so many more of my religious education, make it difficult to judge other systems of belief opposing Christianity.

It is in this lack of absoluteness that I find freedom to listen, learn, and create community of those who practice a creed not of my own, "I . . . suppose."

P.S.
To be continued . . .

Are you curious?

Date: _____

THE AMBIGUOUS REMINDER

MARCH 27, 2020

"Not forsaking the assembling of yourselves, as the manner of some is . . ."

Never mind the often misquoting of this verse; "Not forsaking . . ." rather than "Forsake not. . ." seems to carry a different tone, reading more like a reminder rather than a rule of law, as often declared by religious influencers using said verse to validate Christians becoming members of churches.

The technicalities of this verse and the perpetual misquoting of it are not the reason for this journal entry. Instead, it is to unpack my curiosity around the box built of these twelve words written in the letter called Hebrews, a letter written for the Jewish Christians living in Jerusalem.

What did it look like for them to assemble?

Were Jewish Christians of that time members of churches?

Did they gather once or twice a week, every Sunday, every Wednesday, year, after year, after year?

Did Jewish Christians meet in a building adorned with crucifixes, thorned crowns, and pierced hands?

Because the Bible did not exist, were they studying the letters sent to them concerning their conversion?

When asked, "Where do you go to church?" the answer is, "I am not a member anywhere." Nonetheless, church membership isn't a bad thing. But referring to this writer's reminder so as to convince believers to attach themselves to one group of the same, meeting more than frequently, just doesn't work for me. This line in a letter is a reminder, as I see it. Lacking details, it does not include all of what many pastors expect of their parishioners.

These twelve words and the voices behind them, once held captive my innate desire for fellowship with humanity.

Ambiguity is canceled.

P.S. MARCH 27, 2020

Inspiration brought to me by the 2020 quarantine of our country and its church.

Are you curious?

Date: _____

ENDURING FOREVER

APRIL 4, 2020

Anything I've learned about the concept of heaven was taught to me by Christianity. I was taught that all will be perfect there—there will be no pain and no sorrow. "There will be no crying there," they said. Heaven is where all of the saints (non-sinners), perfected in their existence, will live forever.

The phrase, "His mercy endureth forever" is found in the Old Testament thirty-five times.

The part of mercy's definition Christianity taught me is that of pity or God's undeserved kindness.

Question: What would be the need for mercy to endure forever?

If Christians, declarers of the phrase, are going to heaven in death, what would be the need for God to show pity or undeserved kindness forever?

Believing that God's mercy endures forever, is to believe the world endures forever. But to entertain such a thought is, again, juxtaposed to the position of Christianity as it relates to the teaching of Jesus' return to catch Christians up, i.e., the rapture.

Did those who introduced the concept of an eternal mercy believe there would be an end to the world? Did they have to live life without the hope produced of the message of Jesus' return, ending all evil and suffering as it is taught by Christianity? The thought of living life without the hope of a savior coming to the Earth, ending it all, to create a new heaven and earth, is abundantly intriguing to me. I was raised around and still maintain relationships with believers who are counting on Jesus to return, praying to be a part of those "who remain," or praying to be "caught up to meet him in the air" while declaring a never-ending mercy that is of God.

Is Jesus returning to take Christians, proclaimers of said mercy, home to the only place perfection exists, thereby making mercy unnecessary or does God's mercy need to endure forever because being human, on earth, will endure forever?

Are you curious?

Date: _____

DON'T QUESTION GOD

MAY 26, 2020

There can be no covenant where there is no communion, no communion where there is no conversation, no conversation where there are no questions, and there can be no questions where curiosity does not exist.

P.S. DECEMBER 31, 2020

Christianity points us to an opportunity called "covenant relationship with God" while it, in large part, admonishes us to abandon curiosity by discarding our questions. But if one were seeking to locate the pulse of my relationship, questions asked of God would offer thriving as the diagnosis of our agreement, i.e., covenant.

I am not *questioning* God; I *am*, *asking* God questions.

Are you curious?

Date: _____

A GREATER REVEAL

JULY 6, 2020

Jesus had not and would not do the greatest of works, i.e., "Greater works than these shall you do. . ."

Is it possible to do greater works than Jesus with minimum revelation?

Revelation defined is a divine disclosure to humans of something relating to human existence or the world—this has been my experience. Adding to this definition, I believe, based on personal experience, that there can be a divine disclosure about God.

(navigating)

The author writes that Jesus, a teenager, told his parents he was about his Father's business, but I don't believe he exited the womb of his mother knowing what his Father's business was. What Jesus believed to be the will of God, that which he considered food, had to have been, at some or several points in his life journey, revealed to him.

"But I have greater witness than that of John: for the works which the Father hath given me to finish, the same works that I do, bear witness of me, that the Father hath sent me."

The works given Jesus to finish had to be deeds and acts reflective of the giver, his Father. The works given of the Father were motivated by the essence and nature of who He, the Father, is. In turn, the essence and nature of the Father were revealed and experienced through the works given.

So it is, if the revelation of works *is* the revelation of God, Jesus experienced that revealing quite often, I'd say.

The same God who revealed himself to Jesus through works has given us works to do, greater works, deeds and acts offering a greater experience that not even Jesus would facilitate and for me, that only means one thing: There can be no greater work than the works Jesus did without a greater revelation of the one who sent him.

But can it even be possible to experience greater revelation of God than one of the most worshipped men in history, Jesus Christ?

Are you curious?

Date: _____

DELIVERED FROM DELIVERANCE

JANUARY 1, 2021

I'd like to be over the need to be rescued.

I'd like to prioritize what I believe to be God's perspective of me if Christianity doesn't mind.

Deliverance, to be saved and/or liberated from, was, when I was growing up, an entire event. I'd compare watching the experience to observing an exorcism of sorts.

Reflecting on the experience of observing other parishioners roll in the floor, froth at the mouth, and speak in voices not of their own, doesn't hinder my pondering the thought of humanity ever needing to be rescued.

Superwoman only shows up when there is a need, assessing an experience needing her ability to rescue. Much like Superwoman, God's assessment of me would have to be that of being in trouble, wounded, or broken to employ His ability to rescue. But what if God's assessment of me, His perspective of me, is that of how He created me to be? What if God has always seen me as whole? What if God has always seen me as complete? What if I have always been free?

(reflecting)

I remember watching the sentencing of a man who intentionally caused the expiration of his entire family; wife, two little girls, and unborn son. This offender's parents stood to address the court, the family of their daughter-in-law, and their son. The overwhelmed mother of the sentenced husband and father, her boy, turned to him with endless tears and said, "We forgive you, Son. We love you with all of our hearts." This mother, the one who birthed the man murdering her grandbabies, never stopped seeing him as her son. She will never see her son the same as so many others may see him, like "some kind of monster." If this mother has in her the ability to continue claiming who she birthed as her boy child, after he has committed such atrocities, how much more would God claim us as His own, complete, whole, and free no matter how we see ourselves, no matter the pain we've caused another?

Where can freedom be found in the never-ending need to be delivered, saved, or liberated from "spiritual bondage", imprisonment, or slavery in some form or fashion? Where is the abundant life in persistently viewing ourselves as bruised, fractured, or in danger? Does the refusal to accept our completeness give us over to anything less than our inherent liberty and eternal prosperity? If we always need to be rescued, when do we have time to manifest as we were created to be? If we are created in the image and likeness of God, when do we manifest as such if we are in a constant state of needing to be delivered?

Harriet Tubman is quoted to have said, "I freed a thousand slaves. I could have freed a thousand more if only they knew they were slaves." Harriet's own experience of freedom began before she escaped those who held her and so many others in captivity. Her freedom was in her place of knowing. Such was the same for those she ushered into the reality of their freedom known. As for those who remained in slavery, they did so not knowing they were slaves because they did not know they were free.

In my knowing, God created me whole, complete, free, and He has never changed His mind, only seeing me as He created me to be. Because I believe it, I'll be it, manifesting experiences reflective of such belief.

Can I be over the need to be rescued?

I'd like to prioritize what I believe to be God's perspective of me *and* others if Christianity doesn't mind.

P.S. JANUARY 24, 2021

While writing this journal entry, I could hear Christianity, loud and clear, declaring, "David said, 'I was born in sin!' " David was speaking for himself, not for me. Although found in one of the most idolized books of our day, David's personal resolve frees me to choose whether or not I want to participate in his self-examined conclusion.

Maybe you believe about yourself as David believed: you were born in trouble, wounded, and broken. But it isn't my perspective or even your perspective that I choose to prioritize. Rather, it is what I believe to be God's perspective of you that I prioritize.

Be the whole, the complete, and the free you were created to be.

Are you curious?

Date: _____

A LETTER TO LOT'S WIFE

DECEMBER 29, 2020

Sis, I am just so sorry.

Really.

I am so sorry the story of your life is that of being human, a woman, a mother, and a wife transformed into a dune, making an example of your humanity, making an example of you looking back. The story is in a book labeled Bible, the authority of a religion arriving long after you were so abruptly transfigured. But it isn't okay with me that thousands of spectators gaze upon a mound of mineral, identifying it as you, presuming God allowed such a tormenting experience for as long as the earth remains.

Believing you loved being a mom and probably looked forward to grandchildren made me sorry you weren't told what would happen if you looked back. I am sorry you couldn't have imagined how one could go from existing as a person to existing as a pillar.

I am sorry for how all of your children may have been impacted by, what seemed to be, the sudden and cruel demise of their mother, for the multiple times your offspring may have had to defend your actions because that's what we do with respect to our parents. I am sorry you weren't around to guide your two girls away from incestuous behavior, all because you didn't know what would happen in response to looking back. For the sake of all your babies, some of who you, quite naturally, may have been looking for in that moment, I wish the new mercies of mornings, the mercy your husband gave thanks for, had been your portion. Most of all, I am sorry Christianity, a people you'd never know, seem to share this story, this narrative assigned to your name, without question, without compassion.

Regretfully,

An Empathic Believer

P.S. JANUARY 27, 2021
Her name was Edith because, without a name, she's just a warning.

Jesus is quoted to have said to his disciples, cautioning them, "Remember Lot's wife." But if Christianity involves having to "remember Lot's wife," I don't want it.

Are you curious?

Date: _____

THE SEQUEL

FEBRUARY 10, 2021

She was a loving mother who desperately needed help, her baby suffering terribly. Being aware of a solution that could end her family's anguish, one that worked for so many others, she pursued that avenue as a viable option.

Upon arrival, mom knocks on the door of solution, desiring to be heard, but was ignored. Because she is a parent, one who carried a baby for nine months, baring her in pain, nursing her in infancy, she persists. But her relentless plea was met with notification that she was not a part of a prioritized people, excluding her child and their need to access peace.

But what if Jesus, the door of solution, had been working the drive-thru when this Canaanite woman approached him about her tormented little lady?

Yes, Jesus eventually grants this mom's request but not before she was reminded of who she was not. This Syrophoenician woman, a non-Jewish parent, found herself being compared to the pets of children, desperately agreeing for the sake of her baby girl who, with every passing second, continued to suffer.

For every minute Jesus hesitated to grant this nurturer's request, based on her difference, the agony persisted for her and her household. But if working a drive-thru, listening only to her request, Jesus would not have sighted this mother's nationality. In a drive-thru, her ethnicity would not have been apparent enough to use the dogs of children as an example to distinguish her from the people his ability was assigned to. When a request is made in a drive-thru, honoring said request is based only on the ability to provide a solution in response and for the sake of this hurting mother, baring the pain of her child minute-by-minute, second-by-second, I wish Jesus had the experience of working the drive-thru.

The question, "*What if Jesus worked the drive-thru?*" was asked because it seemed to me that the experience of working in a drive-thru is most like what God, of whom Jesus points his people to, expects of us relating to how to treat each other, no matter our differences. But in the case of the Syrophoenician mother, what is to be done when it is Jesus who needs to be blinded to whom is on the other side of a need?

What if, just what if, it is Jesus who needed the experience of working the drive-thru?

Are you curious?

Date: _____

NEVER?

FEBRUARY 27, 2021

When a friend mentions that which we have heard all of our church lives, "I never knew you: depart from me, you who work of iniquity," my mind packs up to travel through personal experience and other parts of scripture.

Where do I start unpacking first?

Jesus was there at the point of creation, Christianity said. Moses, the author of the first book of the King James Bible, didn't identify Jesus as one of the "us" but the Christian religion taught me that the us, "the Trinity," referred to in the first and third chapters of Genesis, include him. More specifically, if Jesus was there, as a part of the Triune, observing the beginnings of creation, surely, we can suppose he was present when God knew Jeremiah before forming him in the womb of his mother.

If the Godhead knew Jeremiah before forming him, all of mankind, having been formed, was known and what a very settling revelation, if believed. To have been known by the Lord before existing as a human is so real to me. I remember showing up to participate in a church prayer gathering, anticipating an experience of God, only to realize I'd been experiencing God all along. Entering the sanctuary, I got on my knees in front of a chair, as is customary. I was there to meet God where He is as if I'd not been known from the beginning. But suddenly, this lifelong practice was uncomfortable. Changing positions, I lay on my back, interlocking my fingers, using them to hold my head off the floor, then crossed my legs at the knees as though I were at a park enjoying the breeze of the spring air. There wasn't a need to go and meet God. He knew me, I knew Him, and this is an eternally irreversible reality, changing the human expression that is Chandrika.

We weren't born into this world *working* iniquity but if, at this present time, I found comfort in lawlessness, warranting Jesus' "I never knew you," then it is that he, Jesus, was absent at the conception and creation of God's idea to make humanity in His image and in His likeness.

Never?

Are you curious?

Date: _____

OL·O·GY

FEBRUARY 26, 2021
Theology [THē'äləjē] the study of God.
Christianity [krisCHē'anədē] study's *studies* of God.

P.S. MARCH 9, 2021
If theology is the study of God, it is only that a few people received the gift of doing so. Anyone who lived life without the Bible as a part of the world, engaging in the notion of a God, documenting the results of their experience and belief thereof, in my opinion, are the "spiritually privileged."

Christianity taught me that the Bible is inherently of God but so much life was lived, so much life was experienced, before it existed, the Bible.

Suppose those who lived before the Bible are the "spiritually privileged". In that case, God is a respecter of persons, despite Apostle Paul's offering of the opposite sentiment, that being, "There is no respect of persons with God."

But if indeed, God does not favor one group of people over another, the gift of studying God belongs to me, it belongs to us all. The gift of studying God without the influence of other studies is mine to inherit, and I wish I'd known that before spending thousands of dollars on an education, pursuing the desire to study God, only to spend several years studying studies of God.

Is theology important to Christianity? It is to me.

It is a daily work to clear away previous examinations, historical investigations, and ancient resolves about the "God notion", seeing that I took them on as a part of my identity. So to attain what I thought was already in my grasp, God·ol·o·gy, I journey.

Are you curious?

Date: _____

NOTE TO SELF

"People in the Bible" were *not* people in the Bible and "Bible names" *weren't* Bible names.

In some cases, social media guides our lives and decisions because we are hyperaware of how indecency can easily be exposed on public platforms. However, for those who lived in centuries "pre-Bible", the aforementioned reality was not theirs.

If much of what I am reading in the Bible actually happened, as Christianity would like me to believe, it is imperative to keep in mind these human beings lived their lives never expecting to be canonized in a book that would become an authority to millions of religious participants.

Mothers and fathers chose the names of their children not because they knew that one day a book, reverenced by millions, would include the names of their babies, but because of what they believed about the future of their offspring. I'd be interested to know how many parents of those children we read of would have given their child the chosen name if they thought generations to come would take the names as inspiration for their own children.

If I'd birthed a son prior to my time in China, his name would have been Micah, named after an Old Testament prophet. So, this entry is not a criticism of borrowing names from the Bible, but rather to offer that beyond or *before* the pages in this book, were the lives and experiences of people. I will never consider the text without contemplating the all-encompassing lives of whom the words are assigned, committing to the study of the person past the pages.

Are you curious?

Date: _____

LET THE CHURCH SAY CAKE

MARCH 19, 2021

Growing up in church meant, for us, often enjoying dinner with other members of the congregation, where various flavors of cake were available as an expected delicacy to enjoy.

If asked, over a piece of pie, I'd choose a piece of cake, a form of sweet food that includes flour, sugar, eggs, butter, oil or margarine, a liquid, baking soda or baking powder. But, it must be difficult to be cake when all of the ingredients needed to make it are organized separately, in *preparation* to be mixed, stirred, moisturized, beaten, and heated, all to become, hopefully, a taste pleasing dessert for those who later partake.

So it is, a cake isn't a cake even when the ingredients are available to make it.

The presence of the ingredients needed to form a cake only signifies pastry *potential*, calling for "-ing" as a necessary additive to morph into its possibility.

The aforementioned fixings must be engaged by an external energy to become the reality called cake. But without the "-ing" element, there is only the *ability* to be cake—"-ing" is *present* action in relation to the time expressed by the finite verb. There can be a "get*ting* ready to", a "try*ing* to", a "mak*ing* ready", a "prepar*ing* to", all relating to the experience of cake making. But unless there is mix*ing*, stirr*ing*, add*ing*, beat*ing*, and heat*ing* of the ingredients, there's no obligation for the ingredients to become a cake.

Flour, sugar, eggs, butter, oil or margarine, a liquid, baking soda or baking powder mix-*ed*, stir-*ed*, add-*ed*, beat-*en*, heat-*ed* not only produce a sweet loaf but the responsibility to satisfy the craving of those who excitedly cut a piece, fork a bite, appreciating the taste sensation that is sweet.

I begin craving and even smelling cake when hearing Christianity make the declaration regarding His creation, "God is gett*ing* ready . . .", God is try*ing* . . .", God is mak*ing* . . .", God is prepar*ing* . . .". Buying into the notion that an eternal God is expressing present action in our lives, in my opinion, only absolves us of the responsibility to be who we were created to be. As long as God is, for example, "gett-*ing* ready to bless us", "try-*ing* to mature us", "mak-*ing* us beautiful", "prepar-*ing* to make us whole", we don't have to be these realities, relieving us of the responsibilities accompanying them. While writ-*ing* this book even, the duty associated with being a published author wasn't mine.

"The Lord is *still* working on me," is a very common sentiment shared. Just as a cake doesn't have to be the complete version of itself until it is made, if the Lord is still working on us, we don't have to be the whole and finished version of ourselves.

For me, embracing the notion of a bountiful God is to embrace my inherent blessedness. Embracing the notion of an immortal God is to embrace my completeness. Embracing the notion of an ageless God is to embrace coming into this world with an unchangeable beauty. Embracing the notion of an indestructible God is to embrace wholeness manifesting in every part of my existence. To embrace the reflection of God that I am, is to embrace the responsibility of being, in the realm of time, His idea of me.

I don't believe God exists *in* the past, present, or future, making it inconceivable to assign "-*ing*" to His being. It is my experience that time reveals the God who creat*ed* this indefinite and continuous duration called life. God *has* done what He "is go-*ing* to do" so let the church say, CAKE!

Are you curious?

Date: _____

KARENA'S QUESTION

APRIL 8, 2021

"If the love of money is the root of all evil, where was evil before money existed?"

P.S. APRIL 18, 2021

If only the Apostle Paul had written the letter he wrote to Timothy, to my cousin Karena for this question alone. The inquiry she posed in response to my recollection of the 1 Timothy 6:10 verse, sent my God-given intellect on another road trip.

In his letter to the Corinthian Church, Paul makes reference to Eve being deceived by a serpent, making it clear to me that he believed in a woman named Eve, of Adam's rib, eating of a forbidden tree called "Knowledge of good and evil." However, if Paul's sentiment about the love of money were true, money, rather than a fruit tree, would have needed to be present "in the beginning", introducing this concept of evil to humanity.

If the love of money is the root of *all* evil, Moses incorrectly wrote the story of Cain and Able. If murder is a reflection of evil and the love of money is the *root* of *all* evil, Cain didn't kill his little brother because God accepted Able's offering but not his.

Because Paul said of himself, "I find then a law, that, when I would do good, *evil* is present with me", isn't it reasonable to assume that, according to the absoluteness of his sentiment about the root of *all* evil, the evil present with him may have been a love of money? Was the sentiment shared with Timothy actually a resolve from personal experience and projection onto the readers of this letter? Did Paul, in his humanity, have a mote in his eye, seeing in others what may have been his own personal struggle? Did Paul's questionable sentiment about money install an undesirable stain on the canvas of our subconscious? In visiting the reality of repeatedly hearing and reading the apostles statement about the root of *all* evil, I find myself examining the relationship I have with money, wondering if the friction caused by desiring monetary wealth while subconsciously embracing that the love of it produced the existence of evil, hindering, perhaps, a full experience of it.

The Apostle often admitted to his humanity despite, what seems to be, religious idolizing of his life and writings. It is written of Paul to have said, "We also are men of like passions with you." He said of himself, "Not as though I had already attained, either were already perfect." Considering the aforementioned, could it simply be that Paul may have changed his mind about the origin of evil? Although money has existed for at least 3000 years now, it would seem Paul believing the love of money to be the root of *all* evil would be to believe money was created when the tree of the knowledge of good and evil was planted. Did his idea of money evolve? More essentially, did his idea of evil evolve?

Just as Paul the Apostle, a mere mortal, assuredly evolved, my cousin has and continues to do so (and this is one of the most important aspects of my being inspired to write about Karena's question). Cousin Karena and I were raised in the same religious culture but we find ourselves often revisiting and asking questions of so much that Christianity taught us. As important as reconsidering may be, I find more value in the *freedom* to look again, having someone to share with that I see something different.

Carte blanche, Karena's question; it must run in the family.

Are you curious?

Date: _____

CONFIRMATION

APRIL 28, 2021

John the Elder, author of the book of Revelation, has transitioned since documenting the experience that inspired him to leave what has become the last book of King James's New Testament text.

B. W. Smith, a Baptist Reverend born in the south, comes to mind when thinking of John the Elder. My dad owned a 1989 cassette tape of Reverend Smith preaching a sermon I listened to often entitled "Watch them Dogs." This sermon was a comparison of personality characteristics shared among church congregants, comparing them to the personality characteristics of particular dog breeds. His story about the "feist dog" is my favorite. I make reference to this exhortation for its inclusion of John as he concludes his sermon because as a child, it is how I learned of the Elder's banishment to an island, "a lonely island," as Smith exclaimed.

The Isle of Patmos, a Greek island, is where John was exiled as a form of religious persecution and his book contains visions he had while in isolation. There are twenty-two divisions in the sixty-sixth book of the Bible where the words *saw, looked, shewed,* and *heard* can be found in any one of the imagery-filled chapters. The verb *saw* is mentioned as a part of John's visional experience a total of forty times—*looked*, five mentions; *shewed*, three mentions; *heard*, thirty mentions.

Only two of the five human senses were active during the experience John writes about, sight and sound. In his visual and verbal prophecy, John never mentions touching anything he saw. In his lifetime, several of the visions, predicting what he

believed to be the future of Earth's humanity, did not material-
ize and it is that reality inspiring my questions and resolve.

As a matter of choice, I'd ask John if in his death, his visions
were verified. I'd ask him if, when he died, he found Jesus seated
at the right hand of God holding keys to the door of death and
hell. When you transitioned from life to death, John, did you
touch the twenty-four elders dressed in all white, wearing gold
crowns, seated on twenty-four individual thrones like many
songs of the Christian faith declare of our everlasting existence?
Did you join elders and creatures saying, "Holy, Holy, Holy is
the Lord God Almighty, who was, and is, and is to come?" Were
the seven seals tangible? Were they opened or closed? John, did
you get to smile and wave at the 144,000 Israelite tribe members? Did you touch the horse carrying the rider with King of
Kings and Lord of Lords written on his thigh and bloody robe?
Because confirmation of prophecy was paramount as a kid coming up in the church, John, were you able to substantiate the
coming down of a New Jerusalem with its streets of gold and
pearled gates? Did you get a sense, after settling into your eternal reality, that there'd be a second coming of Jesus Christ to
the Earth and what it may be like?

Mama said, "You can't preach what you've not experienced,"
and to declare much of John's unconfirmed prophecy would
be to offer promise where there is no confirmation. Assuredly,
there are those who have gone on to experience life beyond
this one; if only those "walls" could talk, for it is *their* unlimited
reality, not ours . . . not yet.

I am resolved in not knowing all of what life eternal will
present, needing less the assurance of an immutable reward, existing as an expression of God's love, in this life, on this planet.

Are you curious?

Date: _____

WAIT FOR IT

MAY 14, 2021

On many occasions, I have heard from Christian platforms, "The whole earth is groaning and moaning, waiting for the manifestation of the sons of God!" This phrase alters and blends two sentiments found in Apostle Paul's letter to the Roman church: "For the earnest expectation of the creature waiteth for the manifestation of the sons of God," and "For we know that the whole creation groaneth and travaileth in pain together until now."

This "summation" of Paul's two-sentence observation of the creature and creation is often referred to in times of natural disaster as if to say earthquakes, volcanoes, hurricanes, tornadoes, wildfires, landslides, droughts, massive floods, etc., are the Earth's groanings and moanings. Likewise, from pulpits, I have heard it insinuated that these phenomena of nature will end when sons of God manifest.

I am not sure Paul would agree with the summation of others reading this particular view of his, but the present declaration of it inspires a few questions. Supposing that the Earth still has not seen at least two children of God, will it ever if voices of the faith continuously declare creations waiting? If Paul had lived during the Word of Faith movement, known for its weighty teaching on faith confession, would he still be giving power to the words *waiting* and *manifestation*? If one shall have what one says and one is consistently saying what Paul wrote because it will forever be bound to the Bible, Christianity's authority, wouldn't the Earth, or all of creation, be waiting invariably?

Regardless of what Paul meant by his sentiment, it is us, the living, that will have what we speak from our mouths, "The whole Earth is waiting for sons of God to manifest!"

As a child of God, words have the power I give them. Therefore, repeating Apostle Paul's sentiment of creation waiting for the manifestation of God's children is not an option for me. I am birthed from the Creator's decision to make humanity and presently revealed as a reflection of His love. Assuredly, I am not alone or must we continue to wait for it?

P.S. May 29, 2021
Aren't those who declare creations waiting for the manifestation of God's children implicating themselves as being exempt from divine kinship?

Are you curious?

Date: _____

THE DISMISSAL OF A DISTINCTION

JUNE 3, 2021

Jesus' refusal of a compliment makes it difficult to join with Christian charismatics declaring the age-old sentiment, "When I think of the *goodness of Jesus* and all he's done for me, my soul cries out hallelujah!"

Matthew, Mark, and Luke mention in their books the encounter of an inquisitive man approaching Jesus, prefacing his inquiry with "Good Master!" The nameless guy was curious as to how to gain eternal life but was met with correction first. Jesus rejects the compliment by asking and answering a question in return. "Why do you call me good? No one is good—except God alone."

Elementary education empowered me with the skill of identifying distinctions and it seems that even Jesus, as an adolescent, may have learned how to recognize or note differences. But what am I to do with the ability to recognize when a distinction is being made? What does Christianity expect me to do with the inability to ignore the clarity with which Jesus identifies himself apart from God? He dismisses any goodness of himself, assigning goodness to one, God, and God alone.

A month and a half into my commitment to reading the Bible in full, I read Jesus' response in the encounter as mentioned earlier, asking myself a few questions: Am I violating the command "Thou shall have no other gods before me?" In my pledge to the worship of Jesus, have I been committing what so many Christians have prioritized in their preaching, idolatry?

Mark writes of the man involved in this exchange with Jesus making the change in response to the correction offered, i.e., "Master." I can't help but wonder how Christianity benefits from dismissing the distinction, without discussion, perpetuating the worship of Jesus as God while he proclaimed himself not to be.

P.S. JUNE 22, 2021

If Jesus is not God, as he distinctly asserted, then he is, at the very least, but no less significant, created in the image and likeness of his Father. In that wise, if God is good, Jesus is and so are we.

Are you curious?

Date: _____

A GOD LIKE THIS

AUGUST 26, 2021

Today I heard a line of a contemporary gospel song which suggests the soul of every child born is lost. The melodically arranged lyric brought to mind King David's self-described sentiment, being born in sin and shaped in iniquity. One of Christianity's foundational teachings is that of the same–all of humanity is born in sin and this is our spiritual inheritance upon entry into the Earth's dimension.

Why?

Why become a parent?

Why partner with God in being fruitful, multiplying mankind in the Earth, if He is sending to you sinners?

Why bring a child into this world believing the soul of your baby is lost when he or she arrives?

Why would a Christian, believing in a place where a soul can burn for an eternity, bring a child into this dimension of freewill, having no control of the choices their baby will make over a lifetime?

If your child is a gift from God, why accept her as lost?

If your child is a gift from God, why not leave him with God? Wouldn't that ensure an eternally saved soul?

Instead of coming together as a community to celebrate the impregnation of a womb, should we be mourning the delivery of the infant's fallen state instead?

So it is, soul-winning begins with believing mothers all over the world have been gifted by Christianity's Redeemer with the opportunity to give birth to the unredeemed and as an ordained reverend of the faith, I came really close to solidifying my place in that oxymoronic race.

For a long time, it burdened me to know my Christian parents live with the concern of their four beautiful daughters, their grandchildren even, spending an eternity in a fiery damnation. As it seems, giving birth to my sisters and me also meant giving birth to the burden of our freedom to choose either to live a life worthy of the reward of eternal life in heaven or everlasting torture. Their fear had become my weight, but after writing this journal entry, I am left with a question (revised) often heard in Black churches: "Who *would* serve a God like this?"

Are you curious?

Date: _____

THE STRIPPING CONTINUES

HI.

I am an unrecoverable stripper.

This process of stripping away religion, I believe, will be a lifelong journey. This trek to freedom requires as much commitment as my participation in religious experiences once was and I am devoted to documenting the journey.

The most theologically educated, the greatest congregational leaders, the most experienced church-going lovers of God, still have questions.

Sometimes, the answers to our questions, are that we have *them*.

God is not afraid of our curiosity, and neither should we be.

ACKNOWLEDGEMENTS

Lord, I am grateful. Thank You for Your love; it has changed my life forever.

I am grateful for this book assignment and the journey to completing it. For my parents and their very rich investment into my siblings and I, for my friends and senior influences, I am grateful. May W. Brand Publishing reap in abundance for all they've done to get my story to the world. Lord, I acknowledge Your goodness reflected in the weight Mr. Carlton Pearson carried while initiating the charge in transparent transition from religion to spiritual exploration, making space for those of us who would come after him. For his curiosity, time, investment, influence, belief and confidence in both my spiritual work and writing, I am grateful.

God, for everyone who purchases and reads this gift from freedom, I am grateful. Thank You that in these pages every reader finds or affirms the freedom ordained for them.

Amen.

ABOUT THE AUTHOR

Chandrika D. Phea is living in empowerment—of herself and others.

Born in Oklahoma City, Oklahoma, Chandrika never dreamed that she would become a teacher. Teaching English at SIAS University in China to the future generation was life-changing. This experience opened Chandrika's mind to travel the world doing what she has been empowered, mentored, and equipped to do.

As a student at Langston University, majoring in Management Information Systems, she also enrolled in ministerial courses at the Judah School of Ministry in OKC to obtain her license in ministry and was ordained by the same school of ministry a few years later. Phea received a Bachelor of Arts degree in Biblical Studies from Beacon University, in Columbus, Georgia. While working toward her degree at Beacon, she became a substitute teacher for Muscogee County School District. She also served as a Young Life leader for Columbus Young Life Urban and volunteered in serving girls' homes as well.

In 2007, Chandrika joined a local Christian mission, conducting neighborhood Bible studies, building relationships with community members, and creating Vacation Bible Schools in the urban areas of Columbus. This partnership with the community proved as preparation for the position she would later hold in China.

The experience of living abroad changed Chandrika's life, giving her the desire to explore the world beyond church ministry. Since returning to the states, her new found curiosity has led to a new passion in physical fitness, wellness coaching, and the outdoors, where she experiences more of Earth's glory.